Integrating the ESL Standards Into Classroom Practice: Grades 9-12

Barbara Agor, Editor

WRITERS

Sandra Briggs

George C. Bunch

Ellen Daniels

Patricia Hartmann

Carrie Lenarcic

William Pruitt

Gwen B. Riles

Cynthia Leigh Ross

Suzanne Irujo, Series Editor

TESOL — Teachers of English to Speakers of Other Languages, Inc.

Typeset in Optima with Dolphin display
by Capitol Communications Systems, Inc., Crofton, Maryland USA
and printed by Pantagraph Printing, Bloomington, Illinois USA

Teachers of English to Speakers of Other Languages, Inc.
700 South Washington Street, Suite 200
Alexandria, Virginia 22314 USA
Tel. 703-836-0774 • Fax 703-836-7864 • E-mail tesol@tesol.org • http://www.tesol.org/

Director of Communications and Marketing: Helen Kornblum
Managing Editor: Marilyn Kupetz
Copy Editor: Ellen Garshick
Additional Reader: Marcia Annis
Cover Design: Charles Akins and Ann Kammerer

ISBN 0-9399791-87-0
Library of Congress Catalogue No. 00130570

Contents

Acknowledgments

This book would never have happened without the eight writers who gave up the summer of 1999 to turn their classroom work into units that we could all learn from and enjoy.

Thanks are also due to Marilyn Kupetz and Ellen Garshick, TESOL Central Office eagle-eyes who found time to teach me as well as edit my work.

Our series editor, Suzanne Irujo, invited the three book editors into the design and decision-making process. She supported, prodded, and sympathized. She is a model of collegial professionalism.

Because we are the sum of our histories, I must also acknowledge Jean McConochie and Jill Burton, who, as mentors for my early writing and editing, still perch on my shoulder as I work.

Last, but always first, thanks to my husband, Stewart, who offered to provide extensive help on this project and actually did provide a little.

Series Editor's Preface

When I first saw a copy of *ESL Standards for Pre-K–12 Students* (TESOL, 1997), I thought, "These are very well done, but how are teachers going to use them?" Working with teachers since then, I've heard them echo those thoughts: "I really like these standards, but I'm not sure how to use them in my classroom."

The four volumes in the series *Integrating the ESL Standards Into Classroom Practice* are designed to help teachers use the standards. The series covers four sets of grade levels: pre-K–2, 3–5, 6–8, and 9–12. Each volume contains six units, some designed with a particular grade level or proficiency level in mind, others designed to span grade and proficiency levels. There are units for very specific contexts and units that are more general. All the units are adaptable for other levels and contexts and include suggestions for doing that.

These units were taught and written by real teachers, each of whom approaches the implementation of the ESL standards in the classroom in a different way. As I worked on editing the four volumes, I was struck by the wide variety of ways in which teachers who work with standards use them to inform their teaching. In describing what skills must be mastered by ESOL students in public schools, the standards become planning tools, observational aids, assessment guides, and ways of understanding language development.

These units also exemplify the strategies that Lachat (1999) recommends for teachers implementing standards-based instruction:

- Organize learning around what students need to know and be able to do

- Enrich their teaching by cultivating students' higher order thinking processes

- Guide student inquiry by posing real-life tasks that require reasoning and problem-solving

- Emphasize holistic concepts rather than fragmented units of information

- Provide a variety of opportunities for students to explore and confront concepts and situations over time

- Use multiple sources of information rather than a single text

- Work in interdisciplinary teams

- Use multiple forms of assessment to gather concrete evidence of student proficiencies (p. 13)

The teachers who prepared these units did so to demonstrate what they did when they taught the units, not to tell others what should be done. The units were designed to serve several purposes. We wanted them to be complete, finished products, usable as they are in other classrooms, so we made them as explicit as we could. We wanted them to be adaptable for use in other situations and contexts, so we included suggestions for doing that. We wanted them to serve as possible models for teachers who want to develop their own standards-based units, so we provided explanations for why we did things as we did.

These volumes expand upon and complement the work contained in previous TESOL standards publications. We have used appropriate descriptors and sample progress indicators as they appear for each standard in *ESL Standards for Pre-K–12 Students* (TESOL, 1997), although we have also created some new progress indicators when appropriate. We have tried to incorporate the assessment process outlined in *Managing the Assessment Process: A Framework for Measuring Student Attainment of the ESL Standards* (TESOL, 1998). Many of the checklists and rubrics used in the assessment sections are adaptations of those found in *Scenarios for ESL Standards-Based Assessment* (TESOL, in press).

A few technical notes:

- In keeping with the terminology used in *ESL Standards* (TESOL, 1997), we use *ESL* (English as a second language) to refer to the standards, the field, and our classes. We use *ESOL* (English to speakers of other languages) to refer to the learners themselves.

- In order to avoid having to repeat detailed procedures for teaching techniques that appear in several units in a volume, we have included a glossary of techniques. Because of this, there is no glossary of terms, but definitions of standards-related terms are available in *ESL Standards* (TESOL, 1997) and *Scenarios* (TESOL, in press).

- All resources and references for each unit are listed at the end of the unit. Writers annotated the resources where they felt it would be helpful to readers.

Our hope in producing these volumes is that teachers will be able to use these units in their own classes and that they will also gain insights into incorporating the ESL standards into other units they may develop. We want them to be able to say, after reading one or several units, "Now I know what to do with the ESL standards in my classroom."

Suzanne Irujo, Series Editor

REFERENCES

Lachat, M. A. (1999). *Standards, equity and cultural diversity.* Providence, RI: Northeast and Islands Regional Educational Laboratory at Brown University (LAB).

TESOL. (1997). *ESL standards for pre-K–12 students.* Alexandria, VA: Author.

TESOL. (1998). *Managing the assessment process: A framework for measuring student attainment of the ESL standards* (TESOL Professional Paper No. 5). Alexandria, VA: Author.

TESOL. (in press). *Scenarios for ESL standards-based assessment.* Alexandria, VA: Author.

Introduction

Standards. Whose standards? For what purpose? How do standards free us? How do they constrain? How can they guide our work with young people?

Each of the contributors to this book has addressed these questions, both explicitly and implicitly. Some writers have been involved in the ESL standards conversation on a national or state level. Some have worked in teams within their own districts, digesting the standards and translating them into classroom practice. Others have done virtually all of their thinking about standards right in their own classrooms. The writers show us that there is no one way to think about standards and that there are multiple approaches for incorporating them into our work.

In virtually every case, the writers have also looked at standards other than those for ESL: social studies, science, and language arts. Along with these non-ESL standards have come broader institutional requirements, frequently including high-stakes testing. In more and more states, simply amassing academic credits no longer ensures a student's high school graduation.

Standards and their corresponding tests—their value, their nature, their application, and even their existence—are subjects of thoughtful debate among educators. Yet while the arguments continue, ESOL students and their teachers face standards and high-stakes testing *today*. Within their first few days of high school, ESOL students discover that they will eventually encounter The Test. They learn that accommodations will be minimal—perhaps a bilingual dictionary or extended time to complete the test. The pressure is on.

Not surprisingly, three of the units in this book reflect the need to prepare students for high-stakes testing in writing. In Ohio, Patricia Hartmann's students study three types of writing in order to prepare for a state proficiency test. In California, Sandra Briggs' students study autobiography as she braces them for the reality of upcoming tests while soothing their anxieties. In New York, William Pruitt's students study "Beauty and the Beast" and engage in the magic of storytelling while practicing the rigorous thinking and writing that they will need for their state's language arts examination.

The other three units weave the ESL standards into the content areas of social studies and science. Ellen Daniels and George C. Bunch show how collaboration between two teachers can produce a community of learners who, not incidentally, become scholars of history. Cynthia Leigh Ross leads her students through an introduction to scientific concepts that apply both within and beyond the classroom. Gwen B. Riles and Carrie Lenarcic build on the cultural diversity of their students for their inquiry into the world's great religions.

The chapters in this book are intended to show some of the multiple approaches for incorporating the ESL standards with classroom planning and instruction. The writers and I invite you to realize your own approaches as you explore theirs and to engage in imaginary dialogues with them as you adapt, transform, and create. How, for example, can an activity meant to reinforce academic preparation (Goal 2) be further crafted to help students use English in socially and culturally appropriate ways (Goal 3)?

The writers of this book will be honored if you recognize similarities between your own professional practices and theirs and if, at the same time, you find yourself discovering new ways of thinking and working.

Barbara Agor, Editor

UNIT 1
Exploring World Religions

GWEN B. RILES *and* CARRIE LENARCIC

Introduction

It is Wednesday, and my class is preparing for a major test the following day. Several students wonder aloud whether they will pass or fail.

Anne, a Haitian girl, says with a sigh, "Well, if God wants it, I'll pass."

Her Chinese partner, Xiao Ling, turns to her and says, "If you study, you will pass. God doesn't make you pass a test."

Anne responds with, "Well, God gave me this brain. He is the one who directs my life. If he wants me to learn something by failing the test, it doesn't matter how much I study."

Xiao Ling gives Anne a disbelieving look. "Listen, Anne, how do you even know there is a God? I think you use him like an excuse, in case you don't pass the test. You have to have confidence in you. I think you can pass the test. You're a smart girl."

By now, most of the class is listening in on the conversation. Another student pipes up, "Xiao Ling, don't you believe in God?"

"No, I don't," Xiao Ling calmly replies. A murmur of surprise ripples across the class.

Anne looks horrified. "How can you live without God?" she asks.

"Do you think I am a bad person?" Xiao Ling asks her.

Context

Grade levels: 9th–12th grades

English proficiency levels: Intermediate and advanced

Native languages of students: Chinese, Spanish, Bangla, Haitian Creole, other

Focus of instruction: ESL/social studies

Type of class: Sheltered content, single class periods

Length of unit: 6 weeks

Anne is clearly struggling. She has been happy to be paired with Xiao Ling since the beginning of this unit because she knows how thoughtful, helpful, and tolerant Xiao Ling is.

"No, you are a good person. But how can you know what is the right thing to do? Aren't you worried about what happen to you after you die?" she asks.

"When you die, you die. That's it," another student offers.

It became clear from the resulting class discussion that, although among those who volunteered their religious affiliation were many Christians, a few Muslims, Buddhists, and a Jew, there were also a small number of agnostic and atheist students in the class. The perspectives and beliefs of these students had not been previously recognized, let alone validated. Most of the students in this class had been together for the whole school year and felt fairly comfortable with each other. But suddenly they found themselves taking a fresh look at each other and communicating with an intensity and focus we had rarely achieved in the classroom.

We wanted to recapture that sense of inquiry and concern, and mold it into a well-rounded learning experience; this unit is the result.

Unit Overview

We began this unit by exploring the meaning of religion and then examined Buddhism, Judaism, Islam, Christianity, Hinduism, and Shinto (animism). We drew from the students' own questions about religion and spirituality, and encouraged them to delve more deeply into their personal attitudes toward and experiences with religion.

The students worked in groups, in pairs, and as a full class to research and share information on the six religions. The ultimate objectives of this unit were fourfold:

1. to show the students the impact that religion, as an institution, has had on the course of human history

2. to bring the religious significance to an individual level and encourage the students to explore their own perspectives on religion and develop a more sensitive and tolerant view of the religious choices of others

3. to prepare some of the students for religion-based questions on the New York State Global History and Geography Regents Examination, a graduation requirement

4. to develop the students' language in the following areas:

   • using religion-related vocabulary and idiomatic phrases appropriately

   • expressing personal attitudes and sharing experiences using the appropriate verb tenses in spoken and written English

   • listening to and taking notes on group presentations

   • writing comparative essays

The unit overview shows the activities in each of the three strands of the unit.

The students produced a variety of written pieces throughout this unit, including journal entries, dialogues, paragraphs, and a comparative essay. Journals and dialogues allow the students to reflect on and question the content on a personal level. An acceptable journal entry or dialogue will reflect the student's comprehension of the content and ability to synthesize and analyze the material. We used a **process writing** approach

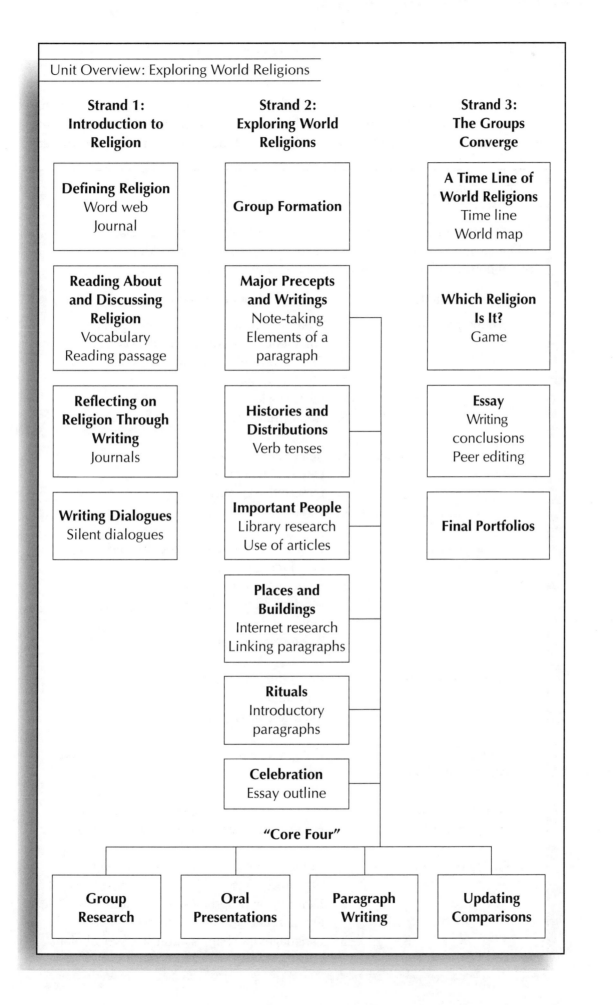

Unit Overview: Exploring World Religions

Strand 1:
Introduction to Religion

Defining Religion
Word web
Journal

Reading About and Discussing Religion
Vocabulary
Reading passage

Reflecting on Religion Through Writing
Journals

Writing Dialogues
Silent dialogues

Strand 2:
Exploring World Religions

Group Formation

Major Precepts and Writings
Note-taking
Elements of a paragraph

Histories and Distributions
Verb tenses

Important People
Library research
Use of articles

Places and Buildings
Internet research
Linking paragraphs

Rituals
Introductory paragraphs

Celebration
Essay outline

Strand 3:
The Groups Converge

A Time Line of World Religions
Time line
World map

Which Religion Is It?
Game

Essay
Writing conclusions
Peer editing

Final Portfolios

"Core Four"

Group Research

Oral Presentations

Paragraph Writing

Updating Comparisons

to teach expository writing and criterion-based rubrics to assess it. The evaluation of group work and oral presentations is described in the sections dealing with those activities.

The portfolio was the final product of the unit. It contained a group-produced chart for the assigned religion, a comparative chart of all religions studied, the comparative essay, the journal, the dialogue, and a visual representation, found or produced by each

Assessment Chart

All student work is assessed with reference to (a) established criteria, (b) language proficiency, and (c) academic achievement. In addition, oral reports involve the assessment of direct performance.

Type of activity	Assessment criteria
1. Writing paragraphs	1. Clear and concise opening and closing 2. Sufficient and correct information 3. Body that supports topic sentence 4. Mechanics and grammar appropriate for language level 5. Appropriate length
2. Writing journal entries	1. Relatedness to topic 2. Depth of reflection 3. Descriptive quality 4. Length
3. Writing essays	1. Clear and concise introductory and concluding paragraphs 2. Sufficient and correct information 3. Mechanics and grammar appropriate for language level 4. Appropriate length
4. Writing dialogues	1. Relatedness to topic 2. Exploration of issues 3. Internal consistency
5. Filling out comparative charts	1. Completeness and accuracy of information 2. Neatness
6. Participating in group process	1. Participation in discussion by all members 2. Fulfillment of group roles by all members
7. Giving oral reports	1. Content: complete, accurate, and well organized 2. Delivery: appropriate speed, volume, eye contact, and audience interaction 3. Language: mechanics and use of vocabulary

student, of the assigned religion. We assessed each component individually and combined the resulting grades to produce the final grade. The assessment chart serves as a reminder for us as teachers. It can also be handed out to the students or posted so expectations are clear. Many students appreciate this help.

Standards

ESL Standards for Pre-K–12 Students (TESOL, 1997) has been an integral way for us as teachers to take a flash of an idea and solidify it into a meaningful, well-organized, intellectually and linguistically challenging unit. Good teaching can be burdensome, tiresome, and sometimes overwhelming. The standards are a neatly bulleted reference we could consult when our ideas were too vast and complicated to make sense. We knew we could never teach everything we wanted about world religions, so we brainstormed dozens of ideas and then used the standards to help create a feasible framework. We then closed the standards book and wrote a unit we believed would challenge our students and ourselves in a meaningful way.

After we felt confident we had produced a well-rounded unit, we returned to the standards. Each goal and standard offered valuable enrichment to our activities. We then added to and modified the activities, using the standards as a guide.

Activities, Strand 1: Introduction to Religion

Defining Religion

Before we begin a unit on world religions, we prepare the students for the unit by activating their general knowledge of religion. This activation process involves encouraging the students to reflect upon their own religion and religious experiences. It also involves discussing key words essential to the topic of religion.

> **Goal 1, Standard 3** **To use English to communicate in social settings: Students will use learning strategies to extend their communicative competence.**
>
> ### Descriptors
> - listening to and imitating how others use English
> - exploring alternative ways of saying things
> - seeking support and feedback from others
> - practicing new language
> - using context to get meaning
>
> ### Progress Indicators
> - ask a classmate whether a particular word or phrase is correct
> - keep individual notes for language learning
> - test appropriate use of new vocabulary, phrases, and structures
> - ask someone the meaning of a word
> - understand verbal directions by comparing them with nonverbal cues
> - practice recently learned language by teaching a peer

For this lesson, we prepare a list of terms related to religion in general that we intend to teach the class.

PROCEDURE

- Activating prior knowledge: First, we write the word *religion* on newsprint and ask the students to think about the concept of religion silently for 2 minutes. We prompt the class with questions such as "What does this word mean to you?" and "What words do you think of that relate to this word?"

The choice of vocabulary depends on the students' language ability and on how deeply we intend to go into content. Choices have included worship, spiritual, ceremony, sacred, pray, monotheism, and agnosticism.

- Developing vocabulary: Working in pairs, the students discuss and write down on a graphic web as many words related to religion as they can in 10 minutes; one pair's web is reproduced here. When the class reconvenes, the pairs take turns writing words on the

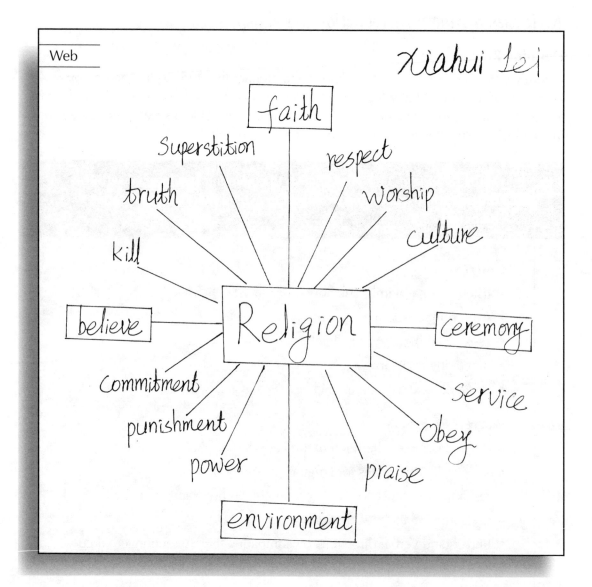

Web

Xiahui Lei

faith

Superstition

respect

truth

worship

culture

kill

believe

Religion

Ceremony

commitment

service

punishment

Obey

power

praise

environment

newsprint. As the students write words, their partners explain why they chose the particular word and how it relates to religion. We then give the class a vocabulary lesson and explain words not yet contributed by the students.

- Writing a reflective journal: The students begin a reflective journal by writing seven sentences, each starting with "To me, religion . . . ."

Reading About and Discussing Religion

The purpose of this activity is to make the students comfortable with words related to religion and encourage the students to discuss the subject of religion using their own impressions and experiences.

> *Goal 2, Standard 2*   **To use English to achieve academically in all content areas: Students will use English to obtain, process, construct, and provide subject matter information in spoken and written form.**
>
> ### Descriptors
>
> - listening to, speaking, reading, and writing about subject matter information
> - gathering information orally and in writing
> - analyzing, synthesizing, and inferring from information
> - responding to the work of peers and others
> - understanding and producing technical vocabulary and text features according to content area
>
> ### Progress Indicators
>
> - compare and classify information using technical vocabulary
> - synthesize, analyze, and evaluate information
> - locate information appropriate to an assignment in text or reference materials

PROCEDURE

- Preparing: We compile a list of all the words from the previous lesson to distribute as a reference guide for the students. We also prepare a reading on the concept and essential function of religion in general. Other teachers may want to modify an already existing passage from an encyclopedia or other source. The reading includes key vocabulary and serves as a spring-board of common knowledge for future activities. We then prepare open-ended questions related to the reading, write them on small strips of paper, and put them into a paper bag.

- Reinforcing vocabulary: We distribute a vocabulary list that includes words, definitions, and sample sentences. The class skims the list and asks for clarification of selected words. The students silently read a passage containing the new words. They meet in pairs to read the selection aloud to one another and to underline or highlight key vocabulary.

- Answering questions: From the paper bag, each student pair chooses a question related to the reading and discusses it before they read it to the class. The questions prompt a whole-class discussion based on the questions and the reading.

Reflecting on Religion Through Writing

Religion can be a confusing and overwhelming subject. When the students are learning about a variety of world religions and at the same time attempting to make sense of their own religious beliefs and experiences, they will inevitably have questions and reflections. We have therefore included journal entry assignments in most of the lessons of this unit. The students can use their journals as a personal forum for introspection and reflection on the various elements of world religions and on the philosophical questions of religion in general.

Goal 1, Standard 2   To use English to communicate in social settings: Students will interact in, through, and with spoken and written English for personal expression and enjoyment.

Descriptors

- sharing social and cultural traditions and values
- expressing personal needs, feelings, and ideas

Progress Indicators

- write in personal journal
- discuss issues of personal importance or value
- reflect on personal experiences centering around the topic of religion

---

PROCEDURE

- Introducing journals: We begin this activity by initiating a class discussion on journals and journal writing. We ask the class to brainstorm reasons people keep journals and invite students who are journal keepers to share why writing is important to them.

- Suggesting journal topics: Because it is often difficult for some students to think of questions or topics for reflection, we distribute a list of suggested topics for journal writing. The topics are broad and philosophical enough to engage students who have not grown up with religion in their lives. Here are some journal topics we have used:

We provide journals (spiral notebooks in various colors) as an incentive for the journal-writing activities.

Describe your religious experience growing up.

What was the attitude toward religion in your family? your community?

How did religion affect your daily life?

Describe your religious holidays and other celebrations.

If you were not raised in a particular religion, how do you view religion?

What is the difference between religion and spirituality?

Do you think technology will influence or even replace religion over the next century?

What happens after people die?

- Assigning entries: We assign two journal entries per week for the duration of the unit. The students receive a set of criteria for journal grading (see the assessment chart on p. 4). Because journal writing is a personal experience, we give the students the freedom to choose from the suggested topics or to write on a topic of their choice. However, everyone completes the first assignment ("To me, religion . . .") and a final journal entry entitled, "How has this unit affected my attitude or feelings about religion?"

Writing Dialogues

When the students are introduced to a large amount of vocabulary, we reinforce their usage and understanding of the new words. The dialogue activity described below is a way for the students to communicate with one another about their religious beliefs and experiences while using and contextualizing new vocabulary. This activity is especially effective for those students who are not yet comfortable with spoken English.

Goal 1, Standard 3 **To use English to communicate in social settings: Students will use learning strategies to extend their communicative competence.**

Descriptors

- testing hypotheses about language
- listening to and imitating how others use English
- seeking support and feedback from others
- learning and using language chunks
- practicing new language

Progress Indicators

- ask a classmate whether a particular word or phrase is correct
- test appropriate use of new vocabulary, phrases, and structure

---

PROCEDURE

- Writing and sharing silent dialogues: In pairs, the students each read their partner's journal entry. On a piece of paper, Student A writes a reaction to

Yelson's Journal

YELSON E. BASTARDO.

MY OPINION ON DEATH, IS THAT YOU GO TO HEAVEN OR HELL DEPENDING ON YOUR LIFE. I THINK THAT IF YOU LIVE A HAPPY LIFE AND DONT SIN YOU'RE GOING TO HEAVEN. BUT I THINK THAT AFTER YOU GO TO HEAVEN YOUR SOUL STAYS THERE TO BE CLEANED AND SENT BACK TO A NEW BODY. AND GOD LOOKS BACK AT YOUR LIFE AND MIGHT LET YOU COME BACK AS AN ANIMAL.

Venila's Journal

Venila Qorhasani

"What happens after we die?"

In my culture many people believe in life after death. I believe that after we die, just our body dies, but our spirit never dies. After death, the spirit goes to heaven, and we have to stand in front of God, explaining our mistakes, and in conclusion, the good and bad things that we have done during our journey on earth, will be counted and from wich we have the most, that's the place that we are going to, hell or paradise (heaven). So hopefully we all will do some good and right things in our lifes, before going to the court. Anyway this is MY OPINION about "LIFE after DEATH".

Student B's journal entry. On the next line, Student B reacts to Student A's comments and responds to Student A's journal entry. The pair continues this **silent dialogue** (see pp. 12–13). After 20 minutes of silent dialogue writing, several pairs read their dialogues aloud.

- Reflecting on dialogue work: The students write questions and comments in their journals, comparing and contrasting their thoughts and experiences on religion with their partner's (see the journal entries on p. 10).

Activities, Strand 2: Exploring World Religions

In Strand 2, each lesson contains activities based on content and is geared toward sharpening academic skills such as note-taking, group work, paragraph writing, and library use. The assessment section for each lesson reflects this dual focus.

We repeat four activities in all lessons in this strand:

1. doing group research

2. giving oral reports

3. writing paragraphs

4. updating the comparative religion chart

Sometimes we vary the order, and sometimes we modify the activities slightly. We refer to these activities as the *core four* for the sake of brevity.

Group Formation and Group Work

Group work, when it is well organized, consistently monitored, and outcome oriented, can be one of the most effective learning environments for ESOL students. There is an increased likelihood that students will call upon their own resources and knowledge to everyone's benefit, particularly when working on a topic such as this one; individual students will probably know more than the teacher does about their own religions. Responsibility for learning is placed more squarely on the students, with the teacher relinquishing the role of expert on the content and becoming responsible for ensuring that the content is ultimately available to all members of the class.

> *Goal 2, Standard 1* **To use English to achieve academically in all content areas: Students will use English to interact in the classroom.**

Descriptors
- requesting and providing clarification
- participating in full-class, group, and pair discussions
- negotiating and managing interaction to accomplish tasks
- elaborating and extending other people's ideas and words

Progress Indicators
- follow directions to form groups
- take turns when speaking in a group
- ask a teacher to restate or simplify directions
- identify factors that inhibit and promote successful group work

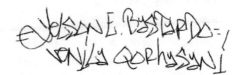

Venila : Yelson, I found your opinion very interesting.

YELSON: BY READING YOUR PAPER IT SEEMS THAT MY CULTURE AND YOURS ARE THE SAME.

Nila: I noticed that too. As you, I also believe that there is life after death. It depends on your life on earth, it depends on how you choose to live your life. What do you think about how to choose your life before death?

YELSON: I THINK YOU SHOULD LIVE YOUR LIFE HAPPY BUT ALSO FOLLOW THE RULES THAT GOD LEFT. DO YOU THINK THIS is RIGHT?

Nila: I agree with you about living happy, but to follow every little Rule, I think for us in this time. It's a little hard, anyway that's what we should do to also have a life in peace in our next "life after death". Your opinion about that God will send us back as people or animals depending on our sins, I think this might be true, but lets hope all of us will come back as people, so please choose to live your life "the right way".

YELSON: I THINK I WOULD LIKE TO COME BACK AS AN EAGLE SO I CAN FLY QUICKLY AND FREELY.

Nila : To come back as an eagle and to fly in the sky, could be a nice feeling, but think about the things that you can do, because there are so many good things to do as a person. Of course you won't fly like an Eagle, but you can fly anyway. I would like to come back as a person, because I would like to do some things that I might not do right now in this life, and maybe because I can't do those certain things. I'd love to try some other feelings or to start a new life and to have new chances, isn't it great to have a second chance?

YELSON: I want to be in touch with nature, don't you?

Nila: I'd like that too, but maybe we could meet again together in the other life, you maybe as a beautiful, strong Eagle, and I as a person. And so you could tell me how it is to fly. I like to fly but not for always and as a person I can still be in touch with nature and I might enjoy it too. So see you in next life, but for right now lets live our life in peace and the "right way", lets respect our lifes.

Earlier in the unit, we distribute questionnaires to collect the following information on each student: name, language(s) spoken, religious affiliation (voluntary), and three religions they are interested in studying. Based on this information, we create a "home" group of three to five students for each of the six religions. These groups (a) consist of students who have expressed an interest in learning more about that religion, (b) are linguistically diverse, and (c) include a practitioner of that religion, when possible.

> Teachers who have less diverse classes or other priorities for their students may choose to form groups in other ways. The teacher can also assign students to groups based on specific criteria such as language proficiency, familiarity with the topic, and personality. Students can also choose their own groups or draw the names of the religions from a hat.

PROCEDURE

- Group formation: For each group, we make a set of index cards containing one card per student. On the front of each card we write a word or phrase specifically associated with the assigned religion and write a student's name on the reverse. After receiving their cards, the students circulate around the classroom, showing each other their cards, to find other students with cards relating to the same religion. When they identify all of their group mates, they sit together.

- Clarification of group roles and procedures: We lead a class discussion of the content of the "Group Roles" and "Group Work Procedures" posters (shown here). Volunteer students read each role and procedure while other students ask questions. We enliven this discussion by asking questions such as "Does the leader do all the work?" "What if the timekeeper doesn't have a watch?" "What if so-and-so always disagrees?" We then randomly assign roles to group members. Roles rotate each time the class starts a new lesson, so each student has the opportunity to practice the skills required by each role.

- Group work: The students have about 15 minutes to produce a piece of group work containing (a) each group member's name and role and (b) one full sentence using each of the words on the index cards held by group members.

- Reports on group work and class reflection: Reporters from each group have 2 minutes each to read all the sentences produced by their groups. We lead a brief class discussion on the successes and difficulties that the students

---

Group Roles Poster

GROUP ROLES

Leader: makes sure everyone has a chance to speak and keeps the group on topic.

Recorder: writes down the findings and decisions of the group.

Reporter: reports the results of the group's work to the class.

Timekeeper/checker: informs the group about time limits and checks the recorder's work for content and stylistic errors.

** Everyone must have a role.

** Roles rotate.

** Roles (except leader) can be shared.

** One person can have two roles (except recorder and reporter).

satisfaction with their two sets of notes based on the increased understanding of note-taking skills developed so far.

- Group research on major precepts and writings: Using new roles and the group procedures already described and practiced, the students discuss the materials they have read and produce a list of major precepts of their assigned religions and a description of the holy writings of that religion.

- Group presentations: The reporter from each group has 3–5 minutes to present the group's findings while the rest of the class takes notes. We take notes on an overhead transparency and share them with the class to reinforce the note-taking skills taught in the previous activities. We take bad notes on purpose, and ask the students to correct them and fill in the gaps. This engages their critical thinking skills and helps put weaker note-takers at ease.

- Comparative religion chart: Once the students are satisfied with the content of their notes, we lead them in transferring the information from their notes to the comparative charts (see the partially completed comparative religions chart included here). We tell the students that we will randomly check their class notes for improvement throughout the unit.

- Paragraph writing: We lead a class discussion about the various elements of a good paragraph based on the class's notes about the major precepts and writings of one of the religions. The students then independently write paragraphs about the major precepts and writings of one of the religions

Comparative Religions Chart

COMPARATIVE RELIGIONS CHART　　　　　　　　　　　　　　　　Name _____

	Buddhism	Christianity	Hindusim	Islam	Judaism	Shinto
Major Precepts and Writings	Eight fold Path. Cycle of rebirth Nirvana text Four noble truth Three basket of wisdom.	Bible Jesus → Son of God Gospel			believe in one god. Old testament Ten Commandment	harmony between People and nature. Sacred (no writing) Kami (many gods) spirit of ancestors
Brief History and Current Distribution	originated from india. 335 million Buddhist followers ↓ monasteries meditation	It spreads after the death of Jesus. Jesus is the long awaited messiah of the Jew.			Live by own tradition. murder of millions in Russia 1900's germany W.WII. nomadic tribes united by kings 1000-900 B.C. live all over.	1880 Ja. Govt. made it national religion.
Important People	Gautama Budha Bodhis sattva	Jesus christ Paul. The twelve Apostles.			Messiah - not yet David → king → nation. Moses → out of slavery & got 10 Commandments	Shrine No established hierarchy. spirits of past People → god.

continued on p. 18

Comparative Religions Chart, *continued*

	Buddhism	Christianity	Hindusim	Islam	Judaism	Shinto
Significant Places and Buildings	- A stupa — containing a relic of Buddha. - Monasteries where monks live.	- Church - The Vatican - Calvary			- Jerusalem — capital city of Jews kind. - Synagogue main temple by Solomon rebuilt	- Shrim. - Amatera su
Rituals	- Meditation - Prayer and Chanting. - stupa.	- The Sacraments - Worship services (on sunday)			- laws for food meat and dairy separately. - Tallith→special clothes. - Pray at sunset on friday. light candles.	- They wash their hand before approaching Shrine.
Celebrations	- Buddha's birthday. - Ullambana Festival	- Easter - Good Friday. - christmas			- Yom kippur. - Pass over. - Roman holiday	- Birth. - Marriage - Newyear - Rice harvesting. - Rice planting.

they are not studying in their groups. We then give the students a sheet with several introductory sentences, concluding sentences, and other sentences, and ask the class to identify which sentences belong to which categories.

Brief Histories and Present-Day Distributions of Major Religions

Religions are not static, monolithic institutions; rather, they have evolved over a period of time and continue to change in our own lifetimes. This lesson puts the major precepts and writings from the last lesson into historical context and makes the connection to modern times and the students' own worlds.

As the group roles rotate during the course of this section, all students give oral presentations of their group's work. Developing criteria for successful presentations is essential to making them effective learning experiences for the rest of the class, to easing the evaluation process for the teacher, and to making grading fairer and more transparent for the students. Student involvement in this process helps clarify expectations.

PROCEDURE

- Evaluating presentations: We ask the students to recall the presentation we gave on agnosticism and atheism and jot down any strong points and weak points of the presentation that they can remember. The class discusses characteristics of good presentations and compares them with the criteria in the assessment chart. The class then constructs a presentation evaluation chart, which we and the students use to evaluate the oral presentations throughout the rest of this strand.

Goal 2, Standard 2   To use English to achieve academically in all content areas: Students will use English to obtain, process, construct, and provide subject matter information in spoken and written form.

Descriptors

- listening to, speaking, reading, and writing about subject matter information
- selecting, connecting, and explaining information
- understanding and producing technical vocabulary and text features according to content area

Progress Indicators

- take a position and support it orally or in writing
- evaluate the content and form of oral presentations
- use content-related vocabulary correctly in oral presentations

Goal 3, Standard 2   To use English in socially and culturally appropriate ways: Students will use nonverbal communication appropriate to audience, purpose, and setting.

Descriptors

- using acceptable tone, volume, stress, and intonation in various social settings
- recognizing and adjusting behavior in response to nonverbal cues

Progress Indicators

- use tone, volume, stress, intonation, and speed in an oral presentation in an appropriate manner for the delivery of content information to an audience of peers
- maintain appropriate level of eye contact with audience while giving an oral presentation
- interpret audience nonverbal response to a presentation and modify characteristics, such as voice volume, accordingly

It makes sense to incorporate student evaluations into the final presentation grade:

1. The teacher is already familiar with the content of the presentations whereas the students are not.

2. Because the students are the ones who must gather content information from the presentations, there are benefits to encouraging

them to judge whether they have learned everything they need to know from the presenter.

3. Teachers often understand their students' speech better than the students' classmates (or the students' bosses or customers, or strangers on the street) do, so they are not always the best judges of students' clarity of speech.

4. Having the students evaluate the quality of a presentation reminds presenters that their true audience is their classmates, to whom the presenters are then more likely to address themselves.

- Completing the core four activities: The students conduct group research on the history and modern distribution of each religion, give oral reports, and update the comparative charts.

- Structuring and writing a paragraph: The students write a paragraph on the history and distribution of a new religion (not the one they are studying or the one they wrote about in the previous lesson), paying special attention to verb tense. Several students write their paragraphs on overhead transparencies in preparation for the next activity.

- Practicing appropriate verb tense use: We collect the overhead transparencies from the students and put them on the overhead projector, one by one, for 3–5 minutes each. The students individually critique and rewrite the verbs in the paragraphs when necessary. Then the class discusses appropriate changes. We encourage the students to write in the simple past tense with some use of the past continuous, unless they are advanced-level students.

Important People

Nearly every religion has important adherents, either historical figures or contemporary ones, who have contributed immensely to its development. Some students may find the religion they are studying more accessible when they focus on real people as opposed to texts, historical records, or statistics. Learning about the lives and contributions of important people shifts the focus of investigation from a potentially impersonal structure to individual human beings. Some of their stories can be quite inspiring.

Studying people also provides a springboard to the library research component of this lesson because biography is one of the main categories used to classify books in the library. In addition, discussion of people and of places requires correct usage of articles. For example, *the Buddha* is correct usage, but *the Jesus Christ* is not. One can go on *a* pilgrimage any time or on *the* yearly pilgrimage to Mecca.

PROCEDURE

- Library research: Each group chooses two significant figures in the religion to research. Each group member brings to the library two index cards, one with the name of a person written on it and one with another topic (e.g., *Vedas* or *monk*) written on it. The students listen to a presentation by the school librarian on the organization of materials in the library and on the correct form for writing bibliographic references. They then work individually or in pairs to find materials containing information about their person and topic. They must find at least three resources, only one of which can be an encyclopedia. On their index cards, they write a reference in

Goal 2, Standard 3   To use English to achieve academically in all content areas: Students will use appropriate learning strategies to construct and apply academic knowledge.

Descriptors

- applying basic reading comprehension skills such as skimming, scanning, previewing, and reviewing text

- recognizing the need for and seeking assistance appropriately from others

Progress Indicators

- select materials from school resource collections to complete a project

- scan several resources to determine the appropriateness to the topic of study

- scan an entry in a book to locate information for an assignment

proper form and a sentence condensing the information they gather from each source.

- The core four activities: The students conduct group research on important people of each religion, give oral reports, and update their comparative charts.

- Use of articles: We ask the students to identify the use or absence of articles in connection with the names and titles of the people they have researched. This task produces a general discussion of the use of articles with proper names, titles, and words that describe what a person does, such as *prophet, savior,* or *teacher.*

- Paragraph writing: The students write a paragraph on an important person in a new religion (not the one they are studying or the one they wrote about in earlier activities), paying special attention to article usage and verb tense.

Significant Places and Buildings

Every religion has holy places, but their number, type, variety, and importance vary from religion to religion. The range from a rock or stream in Shinto to the elaborate cathedrals of Europe is immense and gives the students concrete examples to compare and contrast. Significant places are often closely tied to the history of a religion and in a number of cases constitute a source of conflict among adherents to different religions. Pictures of significant places and buildings are readily available on the Internet, which may guarantee a measure of success in the Internet research phase of this lesson.

PROCEDURE

- Class brainstorm: The students brainstorm and then list types of places that are considered holy space in the religions they are familiar with. This activity reinforces vocabulary such as *shrine, temple,* and *church.*

Goal 2, Standard 3 To use English to achieve academically in all content areas: Students will use appropriate learning strategies to construct and apply academic knowledge.

Descriptors

- applying basic reading comprehension skills such as skimming, scanning, previewing, and reviewing text
- recognizing the need for and seeking assistance appropriately from others

Progress Indicators

- select materials from the Internet to complete a project
- scan several resources to determine their appropriateness to the topic of study
- scan a World Wide Web site to locate information for an assignment

- Introduction to the Internet and Internet research: We take the students to the school library, where eight computers are hooked up to the Internet. We explain and discuss important concepts in doing Internet research. For example, it is possible to find things on the Internet that would be difficult to locate in book format; we recently accessed pictures of ancient Mayan and Aztec manuscripts. On the other hand, there are no standards for accuracy in Internet publishing, so whenever possible, students should try to verify the information they find on the Internet through a print source. We then show them how to log on, and each group goes to a computer station. Once everyone is logged on, we visit a few sites together to get a feel for the Internet and the kinds of information available. Then each group searches for information about the significant places and buildings particular to the religion under study, printing out appropriate Web pages as they go. The students add this material to their group packets.

- Paragraph connections: The students choose one of the three paragraphs they have produced on major precepts, history, or important people and write a paragraph on significant places in the same religion. The whole class discusses ways paragraphs could be connected, using phrases such as *in the previous paragraph* or *as I have shown,* or sentences such as *holy people are usually associated with sacred places.* The students then connect the new paragraph to the three they have already written.

- Information gathering and reports: The students conduct group research on important people of each religion, give oral reports, and update their comparative charts.

Rituals

Rituals give structure to a religion and help maintain its uniqueness. They range from simple to complex and from private to public. Some, such as prayer and initiation into the religion, are common across religions. Others, such as breaking a glass during a wedding ceremony, are specific to one religion. Learning about the rituals associated with a religion can give the students a deeper understanding of what its adherents consider important and how that faith is expressed.

> *Goal 3, Standard 2* To use English in socially and culturally appropriate ways: Students will use nonverbal communication appropriate to audience, purpose, and setting.

Descriptors

- interpreting and responding appropriately to nonverbal cues and body language
- recognizing and adjusting behavior in response to nonverbal cues

Progress Indicators

- compare body language norms among various cultures represented in the classroom or community
- identify nonverbal cues that cause misunderstanding
- describe intent by focusing on a person's nonverbal behavior
- add gestures to correspond to a verbal narrative of a ritual
- demonstrate an understanding of rituals/customs of other religions

PROCEDURE

- Defining ritual: We ask the class for a definition of ritual or examples of rituals. Several students are always willing to give examples of rituals in their own religions and to explain their significance. We ask questions such as "What parts of a ritual can change?" "Who can participate in a ritual?" "Does anyone have a daily ritual, such as brushing your teeth, then taking a shower, and then having a glass of orange juice in the morning, no matter what?" From this discussion we derive a definition of ritual that captures the basics while allowing for variations among the religions.

- Completing the core four activities: The students conduct group research on important people of each religion, give oral reports, and update their comparative charts.

- Writing the introductory paragraph: We tell the students that they are going to write a five- to eight-paragraph essay using what they have learned in class. They have a choice of (a) comparing one topic, such as important people, across the six religions, or (b) writing about all topics with reference to a single religion different from the one they have been researching. We give the students 5 minutes to consider what they have learned in class so far and make a decision on their essay topic. Then we lead the students through process writing procedures to produce their own introductory paragraphs.

Celebrations

Celebrations are the lighter side of the rituals studied in the previous lesson. Celebrating in the classroom is a positive capstone to the long and somewhat arduous learning process. Nearing the end of Strand 2 of the unit, both teacher and students may well be at a point in the learning process where they feel the need for a break in the routine and could benefit from taking a step back to confirm and enjoy their progress.

Goal 1, Standard 2 **To use English to communicate in social settings: Students will interact in, through, and with spoken and written English for personal expression and enjoyment.**

Descriptors

- describing, reading about, or participating in a favorite activity
- sharing social and cultural traditions and values
- expressing personal needs, feelings, and ideas

Progress Indicators

- write in a diary or personal journal and share the results
- discuss issues of personal importance or value
- talk about a favorite food or celebration

Goal 3, Standard 3 **To use English in socially and culturally appropriate ways: Students will use appropriate learning strategies to extend their sociolinguistic and sociocultural competence.**

Descriptors

- observing and modeling how others speak and behave in a particular situation or setting
- seeking information about appropriate language use and behavior
- self-monitoring and self-evaluating language use according to setting and audience
- analyzing the social context to determine appropriate language use

Progress Indicators

- interpret meaning through knowledge of cultural factors that affect meaning
- rephrase an utterance when it results in cultural misunderstanding
- test appropriate use of newly acquired gestures and language

PROCEDURE

- Sharing journals, questions, and reflections: In their groups, the students each choose a journal entry to read aloud and discuss. The students have the option of recording elements of the group discussion or their reactions to the discussion in their journals.

- Completing the core four activities: The students conduct group research on important people of each religion, give oral reports, and update their comparative charts.

- Discussing the final essay assignment: We distribute an outline handout and demonstrate briefly how we would outline each of the two essays for which we have previously written introductory paragraphs. The students then outline their own essays. We also discuss the format for the concluding paragraph. The students write the essay over several days at home and bring in their first draft for peer editing and teacher feedback in Strand 3 of the unit.

- Preparing celebrations: Each group prepares a model celebration or aspect of a model celebration from the religion being studied to present to the class. For this activity, we encourage the groups to include in their preparation classmates who are practitioners of the religion by asking them for assistance in choosing an appropriate celebration and for information on how it is performed. We urge groups to make sure their presentation will not offend any practitioners of the religion they were presenting in this manner but will instead be a joyful experience for everyone involved. When appropriate, the students share costumes, food, rituals, music, and so forth. This is the enjoyable conclusion to a very intense period of study!

Activities, Strand 3: The Groups Converge

In Strand 2 of this unit, the students worked in groups to examine selected world religions and then shared their research with the class. By the end of the seven lessons, the groups have completed a chart of key elements of their assigned religion and a comparative chart of all of the religions studied. Strand 3 reinforces content and vocabulary. The students refine and edit final essays, finish the journals, and assemble the final portfolio.

A Time Line of World Religions

Although the activities in Strand 2 give the students a general foundation on some of the world's most prevalent religions, it is difficult for many students to visualize how the individual religions relate to the course of human history. To help the class understand how the religions fit together in the context of history, they create and display a time line.

PROCEDURE

- Creating a time line segment: We give each group a sheet of newsprint with a line drawn across the center and a set of colored markers. We assign each group a period on the time line to complete, using the "Brief History" section of their comparative charts and using a specific color for each religion. The groups highlight major events for each religion represented within their period of time. (We find that some groups end up highlighting

Goal 2, Standard 1 To use English to achieve academically in all content areas: Students will use English to interact in the classroom.

Descriptors

- requesting and providing clarification
- negotiating and managing interaction to accomplish tasks
- elaborating and extending other people's ideas and words

Progress Indicators

- ask a teacher or peer to confirm one's understanding of directions to complete an assignment
- request supplies to complete an assignment
- use polite forms to negotiate and reach consensus
- negotiate cooperative roles and task assignments
- share classroom materials and work successfully with a partner or group

only one religion whereas others highlight many, depending on the time period for which they were responsible.) The highlights include brief descriptions of events as well as photos and drawings of people and places related to the individual religions. Each group gives its newsprint sheets to another group to examine and check.

- Producing a comprehensive class time line: The class then works to attach the time periods together to form one long time line that we display on the wall. The final product is a time line reflecting the major historical events of six world religions, each in a separate color.

- Clarifying geography: Finally, we place a world map on the wall above the time line with the names of the six religions around the map. Each group uses a colored string and thumbtacks to connect the religion it has been studying to the various places in the world where that religion is common.

Which Religion Is It? A Game

This unit presents a complexity and vastness that may at times seem frustrating and overwhelming to even the most dedicated student. For this reason, we break up the unit with this game as a way to provide some fun and excitement while reinforcing the topic of religion. It is also a good way to synthesize and reinforce content and vocabulary.

For this lesson, we collect a variety of quotes, pictures, and, if possible, objects relating to the various religions. We also consider what kinds of prizes would be appropriate for the winners of the game. The kinds of prizes that seem appropriate vary from year to year and from class to class.

> *Goal 2, Standard 2* **To use English to achieve academically in all content areas: Students will use English to obtain, process, construct, and provide subject matter information in spoken and written form.**

Descriptors

- comparing and contrasting information
- representing information visually and interpreting information presented visually
- demonstrating knowledge through application in a variety of contexts

Progress Indicators

- compare and classify information using technical vocabulary
- synthesize, analyze, and evaluate information
- define, compare, and classify objects

PROCEDURE

- World religions quiz game: We post the names of the six religions on the blackboard, divide the class randomly into groups of four students, and explain the rules of the game. We hold up various phrases, pictures, and objects related to the six religions. These include quotes by revered figures, holy books, religious icons, and photos. Each group has a turn at identifying the religion associated with the object, picture, or phrase.

- The game as assessment: If the group is correct, those students are given the object, picture, or phrase. If they are wrong, the next group gets a chance to guess. The group that holds the most objects by the end of the game is crowned champion.

Essay Conclusions and Peer Editing

Over the course of this unit, the students have worked on drafts of paragraphs and a comparative essay. A lesson on conclusions therefore seems appropriate at this point. We encourage the students to reread and refine their own work using comments generated by their peers. We also meet with individual students for conferences on problem areas on the students' first drafts.

PROCEDURE

- Criteria for a successful conclusion: We discuss the significance of the conclusion paragraph in essay writing. On the overhead projector, we show the class several conclusions for essays and ask them to give reasons they feel certain conclusions are stronger than others. The students write concluding paragraphs for their own comparative essays.

- Peer editing: The students meet in groups of four. They exchange and comment on one another's conclusions. They choose one conclusion to read aloud to the class. The students then carefully read each other's completed essays and write comments, questions, and suggestions on a separate half-sheet of paper.

Goal 2, Standard 3   **To use English to achieve academically in all content areas: Students will use appropriate learning strategies to construct and apply academic knowledge.**

Descriptors

- applying self-monitoring and self-corrective strategies to build and expand a knowledge base
- evaluating one's own success in a completed learning task
- recognizing the need for and seeking assistance appropriately from others

Progress Indicators

- evaluate a written assignment using rating criteria provided by the teacher
- rephrase, explain, revise, and expand oral or written information to check comprehension

Final Portfolios

The final portfolio is the summative assessment for the world religions unit. It includes journal entries, the dialogue, paragraphs, the comparative essay, individual group charts, the oral report assessment rubric, and the comparative chart. The students compile edited versions of each section of the portfolio and submit the finished product.

Goal 2, Standard 2   **To use English to achieve academically in all content areas: Students will use English to obtain, process, construct, and provide subject matter information in spoken and written form.**

Descriptors

- comparing and contrasting information
- listening to, speaking, reading, and writing about subject matter information
- gathering information orally and in writing
- selecting, connecting, and explaining information
- analyzing, synthesizing, and inferring from information

Progress Indicators

- synthesize, analyze, and evaluate information
- locate information appropriate to an assignment in text or reference materials
- research information on academic topics from multiple sources
- construct a chart or other graphic showing data
- edit and revise own written assignments

PROCEDURE

- Putting the pieces together: We choose to give the students a free period during which they can elect to work on any or all of the required assignments for the final portfolio. It is a quiet way for the class to end a challenging unit, tie things together, and reflect on what they have learned about religion, their peers, and themselves.

- Sharing as a group: At the end of the period, we ask the class to sit in a circle. Each student shares an inspirational idea, a reflection, or a memorable moment taken from this unit on world religions.

RESOURCES AND REFERENCES

Classroom Resources

Bauker, J. (1997). *World religions: The great faiths explored and explained.* New York: DK Publishing.

> *Featuring sections on major religions, including ancient and native religions, this work includes religion time lines and maps, graphic descriptions of religious art, and great photos.*

Breuilly, E., O'Brien, J., & Palmer, M. (1997). *Religions of the world: The illustrated guide to origins, beliefs, traditions and festivals.* New York: Facts on File.

> *This work provides a comprehensive overview of origins, prophets and people, writings, places, and rituals and celebrations; it includes excellent photos and graphics.*

Richards, C. (Ed.). (1997). *The illustrated encyclopedia of world religions.* Shaftesbury, England: Element Books.

> *This encyclopedia gives clear, brief descriptions of various elements of world religions. Examples include life-cycle rites in Shinto, Holy Communion in Christianity, and meditation and spirituality in Buddhism.*

Holy Writings

Bhagavad Gita (C. Isherwood & S. Prabhavanada, Trans.). (1987). Hollywood, CA: Vedanta Press.

> *The* Bhagavad Gita *is the most important and influential of all Hindu writings.*

The Koran (N. J. Dawood, Trans.). (1997). New York: Penguin Books.

> *The* Koran *is the Islamic holy book.*

The Torah: The five books of Moses. (1992). New York: The Jewish Publication Society of America.

> *The* Torah *is the holy book of Judaism.*

Teacher References

Levinson, D. (1996). *Religion: A cross-cultural dictionary.* New York: Oxford University Press.

> *This work includes key dates, history, and excerpts from writings on various religions.*

Oxtoby, W. G. (Ed.). (1996). *World religions: Western traditions.* New York: Oxford University Press.

> *This teacher reference provides key dates, history, and excerpts from writings on various religions.*

TESOL. (1997). *ESL standards for pre-K–12 students.* Alexandria, VA: Author.

UNIT 2
Using Story to Compare, Conclude, and Identify

WILLIAM PRUITT

Introduction

This unit is about story and how it helps create a richness of authentic interaction.

> *Eight students are watching a video of Disney's* Beauty and the Beast *(Ashman, Hahn, Truesdale, & Wise, 1991). Within 5 minutes of the opening, they begin making unprompted remarks.*
> Jessica: *Hey, she's not rich.*
> Arijana: *Yeah, and it looks like there aren't any brothers and sisters either.*
> Shanky: *Her father's no successful businessman.*
> Izebela: *They don't live in the woods. They live right in town.*

This unit is about language and the way story shows the twists and bends of language. In doing so, it dramatizes for ESOL students both the uses of language in revealing and hiding, and the meaning that language points to: a gesture made most compellingly in the context of story.

> Dearest Beauty . . . do not let yourself be deceived by appearances. (Lang, 1965, p. 110)

Context

Grade levels: 5th–12th grades

English proficiency levels: Low intermediate–intermediate

Native languages of students: German, Hindi, Vietnamese, Portuguese, Italian, Serbo-Croatian

Focus of instruction: ESL

Type of class: Intensive English, 120 minutes per day (includes social studies as content)

Length of unit: About 2 weeks, with some readiness activities in the weeks preceding the unit

---

Trust your heart and not your eyes
Appearances are full of lies. (Gerstein, 1989, n.p.)

Unit Overview

As a sometime professional storyteller turned full-time teacher, I am a true believer in the uses of storytelling and the value of story in all areas of learning. Many qualities of storytelling are self-evidently classroom-friendly: Students are engaged, the teacher/teller bonds with the students, the content achieves the discrete form it needs in order to be retained, and, crucial in the ESL classroom, the students are encouraged to speak to a group themselves both for communication and for aesthetic effect. Unlike dramatic recitation, storytelling requires the audience's moment-to-moment understanding before moving on to the next scene. One of the interesting effects of storytelling on an audience is that, after the telling, the listeners themselves become more gregarious, sociable, and talkative. Storytelling is infectious.

Again unlike some forms of repetition or dramatic recitation, storytelling is not about creating a sense of awe over the performer or the performer's abilities. It is about passing something along, the transmission of which creates great excitement and a desire to do the same—to give something meaningful. For me, storytelling is about sharing dialogue as much as anything. I want to make sure my students have plenty of opportunities to experience story. I tell them my own stories, stories from history, traditional stories that I have worked on and polished, and stories about what happened to me on the way to school. And I make sure that the students have plenty of opportunities to do the same. I block out time and give rewards and various enticements for telling stories of all kinds.

To tell a story is to internalize speech. One cannot acquire a story, just as one cannot acquire a language, by "learning" it, that is, by consciously memorizing it or otherwise learning it by an act of will. The story must speak to the listener, and the listener must then take the story into the heart, where, if it resonates, it may in turn find expression in the words of the new teller. Because a good story speaks not to the consumer—not to the mass student—but to each person, individual students may internalize the story in ways that they will do with little else heard in the course of the school day.

A third quality that makes storytelling a vital part of learning is the activity's capacity for demonstrating the malleability of language. No two people tell the same story in the same way. It is an axiom in storytelling that what the teller says must be in his or her own words. Strictly speaking, even one teller will not tell the same story twice in exactly the same way. Subtle modifications based on the audience's needs and the teller's insights make storytelling a much more plastic event in terms of language than, for instance, a play.

In this way, different versions of the same story show the second language learner how language may be modified to suit the occasion. One may say that the sequence of events is the constant, and the local conditions such as language and culture are the variable. Thus storytelling is an engaging, meaningful, and educational constant upon which to hang the well-worn hat of language.

Finally, how can the study of story help the students with critical thinking? I use the term *critical thinking* in two senses: first, the ability to compare and contrast, as well as to draw conclusions, in an academic setting such as a statewide standardized test; and, second, the capacity to survive everyday life by learning to analyze the onslaught of sense-impressions, especially by the media. This pressing need of everyone, especially children, to learn how to deal with the assault on the senses by electronic media first led me to the unit "Beauty and the Beast."

The goals of the unit are as follows. Students will

- understand the different uses of story—for education, entertainment, and persuasion—and indicate their understanding by producing stories through remembering, reciting, writing, and telling

- understand the use of metaphor in a variety of literary forms and demonstrate their knowledge by writing with metaphor

- become familiar with how the same story may differ as it appears in different perspectives, media, and cultures, and compare and contrast these forms

- learn how to examine critically the presentation of story for meaning by comparing different versions and learn to draw conclusions about the meanings of these differences

The unit overview shows how receiving the experience of story helps learners connect the strange with the familiar and ultimately helps learners tell their own stories.

Standards

For me, the best way to plan is to conceive of the activity in and of itself, without reference to extrinsic factors. The best activity will reach across the broadest range of educational needs. As I see them, the standards are there to help teachers confirm and clarify but not to inspire. Upon reviewing *ESL Standards for Pre-K–12 Students* (TESOL, 1997), I found it heartening to see that this unit addresses such a wide variety of goals; it gave me a sense that I was on the right track. In addition, looking at the standards helps me think analytically about what I am doing as a teacher, something I am not often inclined to do. In other words, looking at my own planning through the grid of standards creates a dialogue between my reflective self and my teaching self.

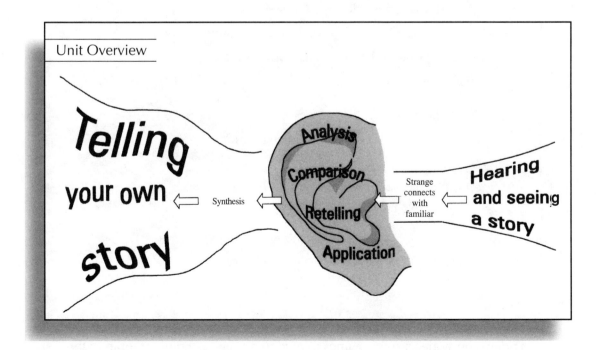

Unit Overview

Activities

Storytelling

Although this unit lasts only 2 weeks, preparation for it includes frequent storytelling from the beginning of the school year. Stories and story sense can find their way into a classroom directly and indirectly in a variety of ways; I find both routes crucial, just as both learning and acquiring language are.

Goal 1, Standard 1 **To use English to communicate in social settings: Students will use English to participate in social interactions.**

Descriptors

- expressing needs, feelings, and ideas
- using nonverbal communication in social interactions

Progress Indicators

- express feelings through story
- engage a listener's attention
- clarify and restate information as needed

Goal 1, Standard 2 **To use English to communicate in social settings: Students will interact in, through, and with spoken and written English for personal expression and enjoyment.**

Descriptors

- describing a favorite activity
- sharing social and cultural traditions and values
- expressing personal needs, feelings, and ideas
- participating in popular culture

Progress Indicators

- discuss issues of personal importance or value
- write a story
- listen to, read, watch, and respond to stories
- recount events of interest
- express humor through verbal and nonverbal means

PROCEDURE

- Storytelling by the teacher: I tell my students stories at least every other Friday. The stories are sometimes related to a specific theme or topic in the curriculum but at other times are not. Here are some pointers on telling stories to the class:

1. Storytelling must not be too self-conscious an activity, either for the teller or the listeners. Try to keep the mood low key and emphasize transmission rather than performance, as good teachers do all the time, talking so their students listen. The only difference is that the talking occurs in a narrative format.

> My students sit on chairs or on the floor, often on pillows or beanbag chairs that are used for reading time. I bring a floor lamp with an incandescent bulb from home because it has a cozier, more informal feeling than the glaring fluorescent bulbs that line the ceiling. It is amazing what a little change in lighting will do for the atmosphere of a room.

2. To enhance feelings of naturalness, always tell the story in your own words, words you would use when speaking to an audience. It also seems to help if the time for telling recurs as a normal part of the flow of events rather than occurring at some special time. Storytelling should even be kind of ordinary, but pleasant.

3. At the same time, be prepared to step out of the "teacherly" role. One of the joys of telling is to let go and focus on the story. That means building a level of trust. You cannot tell a story properly if you are worried about what people are doing. If you can, delegate that responsibility to another teacher or an aide. If you cannot, simply say, "I can't tell the story if there are other things going on." The first rule is respect. Negotiate a way that works for you, but do not sacrifice the story. If you have to center on keeping things out, you cannot let the spirit of the story in.

- Activities that could lead to storytelling: A good way to introduce storytelling is to have the students do it without realizing they are telling stories. This is possible if you emphasize remembering and problem solving rather than performing. For example,

1. Have the students pair off and take turns telling each other a story that they have just heard someone else tell.

2. To solve a complex problem, start a story and have the students write a conclusion that satisfies the contingencies of the story. Then encourage them to read their conclusion aloud. In this way, reading becomes telling.

> A caveat: In listening to stories, teenagers especially may feel estranged if the event reminds them of something too oriented to early childhood.

3. If you are doing a unit on objective reporting, have the students write about an accident they witnessed and read it aloud. This work becomes storytelling through the students' own desire to communicate and their listeners' natural curiosity.

- Actual storytelling: I make sure to allow time for the students to tell their own stories, both formally (if they want to model some of the telling they have either seen me do, or heard others perform on tape) and informally. I look for ways in which informal storytelling can enrich the language base of the classroom.

Finding the Moral

More formal preparation for this 2-week unit begins with a study of Aesop's fables. I used to look down on Aesop's fables as literature, considering them didactic, narrow, and somewhat shallow. But as the basis for a classroom exercise, the fables have some surprising benefits. I use a version I found in the library (Lawrence, 1997) that has a generous selection of fables written in colloquial contemporary English as opposed to one in my own classroom library, which contains just a few selections written in a stilted, "literary" style.

Goal 2, Standard 2   To use English to achieve academically in all content areas: Students will use English to obtain, process, construct, and provide subject matter information in spoken and written form.

Descriptors

- retelling information

- selecting, connecting, and explaining information

- analyzing, synthesizing, and inferring from information

- responding to the work of peers and others

- demonstrating knowledge through application in a variety of contexts

Progress Indicators

- synthesize, analyze, and evaluate information

- explain change in characters in literature

- use contextual cues

Procedure

- Find the moral: I put each fable on an overhead transparency without the moral, ask the students what the moral is (once they understand the concept), and watch the fun. This activity is surprisingly difficult and complex; the succinctness of the fable form itself makes it very useful in ESL. The conceptual and linguistic constraints involved in putting into one sentence

Another valuable quality of the fables is that the act of finding the moral calls attention to the story itself (rather than to discrete events in the story) in a way that encourages the kind of critical thinking so increasingly favored in standards and tests. In this case, the attention to form is intrinsic to the nature of the story. It is the story that asks rather than a teacher or study guide proposing the usual school questions.

the lesson, or moral, of the story can be a challenge for even advanced-level English learners.

- Write a story: Once I have collected a sufficient quantity of stories with morals, I pair the students and ask each pair to choose a moral and come up with a story to illustrate it. When the students read their stories aloud, the others try to guess which moral the story is illustrating.

- Explore metaphors: I use the explanation of the moral as a step-by-step explication of the process of metaphor, an especially valuable feature when the students may not have a clear concept of metaphor. For example, if we demonstrate that in the fable "The Fox and the Grapes" the fox decides or says he does not want the grapes because he cannot get to them, it is only a short step to the grapes being a metaphor for what one cannot have and, further, to *sour grapes* being a metaphorical idiom. These fables are an excellent introduction to allegorical thinking and symbolic representation.

If you find yourself running out of Aesop's fables, simple proverbs work equally well, as the following story, written by a student, attests:

A man brought home a tiger cub. His wife said, "Take it away. It's not good to have it here." But the man wouldn't listen. Then one day he came home to find his wife and child dead, killed by the tiger.

The student had taken the proverb a stitch in time saves nine.

Other story-related metaphorical idioms are
- cry wolf
- don't kill the goose
- the leopard couldn't change his spots
- wolf in sheep's clothing

Reading the Story

Next comes a formal introduction to the unit (what the class will be studying and why), followed by the reading of the text of "Beauty and the Beast" itself. I use a version from *The Blue Fairy Book*, one of a series edited by Lang (1899/1965), that was translated from the French.

I had wanted to do this lesson for some time before I tried it. This was the class I felt it was most appropriate for: young, receptive to story, and mostly female. I explained that our purpose was to critically examine different versions of the story and, further, that the new versions of the New York State Regents examinations were stressing critical thinking and writing. Thus, I was able to use the new tests themselves to create an authentic sense of urgency (in both myself and the students), and I

A good unit is not strictly limited by gender and age. Two boys in that first class showed considerable enthusiasm. I have also used the unit with classes of teenagers and adults, who showed vigorous involvement. The key factors are the existence of narrative tension in the story (whether it is The Three Little Pigs or The Iliad) and the main character's breadth of appeal. At the important moments of the story, boys as well as girls can identify with Beauty because her actions are not exclusively defined by gender. (In other words, she is not Barbie.)

was able to give them license to enjoy a "children's story" that was at least somewhat familiar to most of them.

Goal 2, Standard 1   To use English to achieve academically in all content areas: Students will use English to interact in the classroom.

Descriptors

- requesting and providing clarification
- participating in full class, group, and pair discussions
- asking and answering questions
- explaining actions
- elaborating and extending other people's ideas and words

Progress Indicators

- join in a group response at the appropriate time
- share classroom materials and work successfully with a partner

---

PROCEDURE

- Reading: With a small class, reading the story together takes about 4 days, spending about 25–30 minutes per day. We take our time; it seems effective in a small class to let people who want to read take turns for a paragraph or two at a time. About half the class reads aloud, plus myself. I alternate this method with having the students read in assigned pairs and check each other's understanding. Knowing they will be experiencing other versions that I have told them will have subtle but important differences, the students listen closely for the content of this version.

- Regular reviewing: Each time a reader finishes, I review the material in capsules to check and verify the class's understanding, often asking questions of individuals. I am careful to do this not in the spirit of catching anyone off guard but to let the students know that (a) we are reading complex material; (b) we are reading language that is different from what we use when we talk, but we can see parallels between this potentially forbidding form of language—Victorian literary English—and the contemporary, everyday oral English with which we can happily communicate; and (c) it is really important that everyone understand the story. I am also careful to not let the questioning and encapsulating process violate or interrupt the flow of the story.

- Assessment: The review and questioning mentioned above is part of a continuous oral assessment that takes place daily. With a small class, I can get a quick reading of each student's understanding regarding the sequence of the story and motivation of the characters, and this becomes an extremely important step in the development of the unit. With a larger class, I would use short daily quizzes to check comprehension.

- Summarizing: To support a collective understanding of what is going on in this first formal pass over the story, every day I create a summary of what we have read and let the class see it in writing, as another way of experiencing the story. The new story is in our own words. I elicit the sequence from the whole class, put it on the board, then type it up and give it to the students the next day. We compare the language and pacing of Lang's version with our own.

> Synthesis is not dumbing down. I want to make sure the students are visualizing, both in time (the plot) and place (the scene). A storytelling teacher once said, "If the audience is restless, it's probably because the storyteller does not see the place where the story is happening." Once the picture is in the mind, you can always fill in the details: gold, silver, furniture, books, precious goods.

Lang's (1899/1965) version:

> But one day, a most unexpected misfortune befell them. Their house caught fire and was speedily burnt to the ground, with all the splendid furniture, the books, pictures, gold, silver and precious goods it contained; and this was only the beginning of their troubles. Their father, who had until this moment prospered in all ways, suddenly lost every ship he had upon the sea, either by dint of pirates, shipwreck or fire. Then he heard that his clerks in distant countries, whom he trusted entirely, had proved unfaithful; and at last from great wealth he fell into direst poverty. (p. 100)

Our version:

> Then one day everything went bad. His big house burned down. His ships that were loaded with goods sank in the ocean. And at the same time, he found that his employees, whom he trusted to run his business, were crooked, and had taken his money.

> If I were to prepare this unit for a class in which there were considerable instances of learning or reading disability, I would replace Lang's (1899/1965) version of the story with my own simplified version, one that could be told in small increments with daily recapping.

Through our regular summarizing, the story is (a) reconfigured in contemporary idiom and (b) greatly consolidated. Through repetition within a variety of narrative contexts, the students are also acquiring language about critical analysis and a synthesis of the important points that make this story what it is.

Listening to and Reciting a Poem

Every week, I give the students poems to listen to, enjoy, read aloud, and, if they like, recite from memory and thereby earn credits. Making poetry a part of the regular class-room environment helps the students get used to the values of sound; part of the reason that poetry exists is so that the sounds of words can be enjoyed. This enjoyment can be an important learning experience for ESOL students, who cannot be expected to under-stand everything they hear and sometimes must simply listen to sound without meaning.

This chore can be a great deal less onerous if teachers show them that the sound of the human voice expressing some kind of language can itself be a pleasant thing. In poetry, we can say, "Just listen to the sound and enjoy."

To love sound is to begin to understand rhyme and repetition. To experience poetry in print is to understand stanza. And the presence of metaphor may lead to the discovery that words are connected to the innermost regions of the heart.

Goal 1, Standard 3 **To use English to communicate in social settings: Students will use learning strategies to extend their communicative competence.**

Descriptors

- listening to and imitating how others use English
- learning and using language "chunks"
- practicing new language
- focusing attention selectively

Progress Indicator

- recite poems aloud or to oneself

PROCEDURE

- Reading a sample poem: During the reading of the text, I give the students a poem taken from a film version of *Beauty and the Beast* (Green & Gerstein, 1992), which they will see later. At this point, they may simply listen and enjoy, read aloud, recite, or begin to memorize the poem.

> Dearest Beauty, have no fear,
> You alone are mistress here.
> My palace, my garden, my roses so sweet,
> All that I have is laid at your feet.
>
> Dearest Beauty, have no fear,
> You alone are mistress here.
> Trust in your heart, not your eyes
> Appearances are full of lies.
>
> Dearest Beauty, the hour is late,
> Happiness won't always wait
> Run to the center of your own heart's maze
> And there find love for all your days.
>
> (Gerstein, 1989, n.p.)

Experiencing and reciting the poem allows several things to happen:

1. It puts significant parts of the story in condensed form and gives the students an insight into the real values of the story; it also gives them

a different way of "participating" in the story, by reciting. Thus it clarifies and energizes the reading process for them at a time when slogging through the text threatens to render meaning opaque.

2. Poetic values create another layer to wash over the prose: The chanting quality creates a tone of en*chant*ment, thus bringing the form closer to the meaning of the story.

3. The students learn about sound, rhyme, rhyming couplets, stanzas, repetition, and metaphor (e.g., "heart's maze") as poetic devices.

- Understanding rhyme: We talk about the sound values of the poem, that is, which words sound alike. One of the most common misconceptions among people who speak only one language is that rhyme is absolute, because a vowel is a vowel. But to a Pole or a Chinese person or a Mexican, *maze* does not necessarily rhyme with *days* until someone says it does. Rhyme depends on vowels, and vowel sounds are much more approximately articulated than consonants. Rhyme needs to be taught across languages, with the understanding that eliciting a student's first guess at rhyming words will need to be followed up with training in how Americans hear rhyme. As the poet Stafford (1978) has said, "All words rhyme, sort of" (p. 26).

- Thinking about form: Because contrast often facilitates teaching, I look at how the poem is unlike a work of prose—where the lines end, what elements the poem has instead of paragraphs, and so forth.

Watching Films

After spending 4 days reading the text, we watch the Disney-produced film *Beauty and the Beast* (Ashman et al., 1991). When I first used this unit, I had my own ideas about what the Disney film did to the original story. I wanted the students to compare and contrast these two versions (with later versions added for enrichment), and I wanted them to draw conclusions from the comparison.

Goal 2, Standard 3 **To use English to achieve academically in all content areas: Students will use appropriate learning strategies to construct and apply academic knowledge.**

Descriptors

- focusing attention selectively
- using context to construct meaning
- taking notes to record important information and aid one's own learning
- actively connecting new information to information previously learned

Progress Indicators

- verbalize relationships between new information and information previously learned in another setting
- rephrase, explain, revise, and expand oral or written information to check comprehension

PROCEDURE

- Preparing: The first time through this unit, I identified and charted the differences between the two versions that I thought were important and revealing and to which I hoped I could lead my students. In summary, the comparison reveals the following points:

Differences Between the Two Versions

In the text	In the movie
1. Beauty's father is a successful businessman whose luck goes bad, and the family goes from being well off to being poor. Beauty has brothers and sisters.	1. Beauty's father is an absent-minded, ludicrous, clownlike inventor, and her family (which consists of just her and her father) is "low class," without any particular change in fortune.
2. Beauty's father is imprisoned by the Beast after he takes a rose from the Beast's garden, intending to bring it to Beauty.	2. Beauty's father is imprisoned by the Beast for trespassing.
3. The father returns to the family, having vowed to the Beast to return after a specified time or have someone return in his place.	3. The horse returns without the father.
4. Beauty returns to the Beast with her father, fully knowing what awaits her. (She insists on going because the rose had been taken for her.)	4. Beauty returns to the Beast on her father's horse with no knowledge of where she is going or what awaits her.
5. We do not learn that the Beast is a man until Beauty learns it.	5. We learn that the Beast is a former (wealthy) man early in the story, long before Beauty learns it.
6. Beauty sees the Prince in a picture and in her dream, not yet knowing his identity.	6. Beauty sees the Prince in a broken picture, in a room in a locked part of the house.
7. Beauty vows to stay with the Beast, and she does, despite her fears.	7. Beauty is overcome by fear and tries to escape, breaking her vow. (The Beast rescues her from wolves but is hurt defending her.)

continued on p. 43

Differences Between the Two Versions, *continued*

In the text	In the movie
8. Beauty misses her father and family, and asks the Beast's permission to return for a specified time.	8. The Beast gives Beauty a kind of magic mirror, in which she looks to learn of her father's sickness and a subplot involving his incarceration by a villainous suitor, Gaston; pitying her father, she asks the Beast to set her free.
9. Beauty leaves her family (despite their resistance) when she dreams of the Beast's need for her.	9. Beauty's return to the Beast happens by accident, based on her showing the magic mirror to the villagers to save her father from them by validating his vision of the Beast, which Gaston is using to demonstrate the father's insanity; her action has the unforeseen (to her) consequence of inciting the villagers to attack the Beast's palace.
10. Beauty returns to the Beast fully intending to commit herself to him.	10. Beauty returns to the Beast only as a contingency, to "save" him from the villagers.
11. The Beast is dying because of Beauty's neglect, which she recognizes.	11. The Beast is dying because of a wound inflicted by Gaston.

1. In crucial places, the movie takes away intention and responsibility, and replaces them with accident, hysteria, and mercurialness (Points 2, 3, 4, 7, 8, 9, 10, and 11 on the chart).

2. The story in the text is about the universality of the events. In the movie, the characters are deliberately idiosyncratic, ludicrous, or otherwise set apart. The events are not about, and they could not happen to, you and me (Point 1).

3. In the text, Beauty internalizes the events though dream and perspective. In the movie, events happen outside Beauty's power and intuition, and even outside her own knowledge, thus splitting the perspective of the narrative from that of Beauty and discouraging the audience from wholly identifying with her (Points 5, 6). In the movie, the story has been taken from Beauty; she must now share it with the Beast.

- Teaching grammar: Before, during, and after this time I do grammar minilessons involving the uses of *and* and *but.* In showing relationships between objects of comparison, the students demonstrate their knowledge of category and an ability to use English to manipulate that knowledge. I want my students to be able to say, "My sister is tall, but my brother is short," thus showing how to use height words for contrast. (See pp. 51–52 for two examples of students' writing with comparisons.)

This grammar minilesson also provides an opportunity to show the students that contrast itself is one of the main ways to evoke meaning. How many times, as ESL teachers, do we simply use an opposite to explain a word?

- Using assessment as learning: After viewing the video, we informally describe some of the ways the text and the movie are the same and some of the ways they are different. After brainstorming and listing these ways together with the class, I give the students a quiz that contains descriptors of the film, and I ask them to complete each sentence with an equivalent descriptor from the text, which they have in their possession.

The quiz creates a scaffolding through language that makes clear exactly what is being compared. I tell the students I do not want simply a negative of the first part of the sentence but a positive counterstatement. Nevertheless, requiring only that they write "in the text" before their answer, I allow them considerable freedom to decide how they will complete the sentence rather than simply creating a cloze activity. I hope that their answers will resemble the information in "Differences Between the Two Versions" (p. 42).

One of the benefits of a test of this kind is that it creates a language pattern of contrast, which the students may internalize as they mediate between film and text.

- Comparing with another version: During the second week, I present two other versions of the story. From the Public Broadcasting System's series Long Ago and Far Away, hosted by James Earl Jones, the students watch a 30-minute version of *Beauty and the Beast* that consists of Gerstein's adaptation of his own illustrated book (Green & Gerstein, 1992), narrated by Mia Farrow. This classy but spare rendition, which is an almost direct retelling of the older, traditional version, would not sustain teenagers' interest on its own, but based on the framing of the story and their work on it, they are interested in its similarity to the text and in its divergence from Disney's film. This version also helps students who still have trouble with the language of the text visualize the traditional story.

Quiz

Beauty and the Beast

Example: *In the movie, Beauty gets on her father's horse, and it takes her to him, without her knowing where she is going. In the text, <u>she volunteers to go back with her father, knowing that she is going to meet the Beast.</u>*

1. In the movie, the horse returns without the father. In the text, _____ _____ .

2. In the movie, the father is imprisoned by the Beast for just being on his property. In the text, _____ _____ .

3. In the movie, we learn the Beast is a man early in the story. In the text, _____ .

4. In the movie, Beauty first sees the prince in a broken picture in a forbidden wing of the house. In the text, _____ _____ .

5. In the movie, Beauty tries to get away after promising she would stay. In the text, _____ _____ .

6. In the movie, the father is an absent-minded, foolish inventor who was never very successful. In the text,_____ _____ .

7. In the movie, the Beast lets Beauty return because she sees her father is sick, and she feels sorry for him. In the text, _____ _____ .

8. In the movie, the Beast has a goofy smile and terrible table manners. In the text, _____ _____ .

9. In the movie, Beauty learns about the place she is away from by looking in a special mirror. In the text, _____ _____ .

10. In the movie, Beauty returns to the Beast after trying to save her father by showing the "mirror" image of the Beast to the villagers. In the text, _____ .

11. In the movie, Beauty's intention in returning to the Beast is to save him from an attack by the villagers. In the text, _____ _____ .

12. In the movie, the Beast is dying from a wound by Gaston. In the text, _____ .

- Studying another variation: As a final variation, I show the students an adaptation of the story, directed by Roger Vadim, from Shelley Duvall's Faerie Tale Theatre (Terry, Fuchs, & Vadim, 1984), in which Susan Sarandon plays Beauty. This version, which is somewhat of a parody, is a good way of closing the unit, although it still presents valuable areas for comparison.

- Evaluating: Through the compare-and-contrast procedure, the students get used to looking at different versions critically and pointing out differences spontaneously. Most can correctly answer at least 10 of the 12 quiz questions. Some of the students' quiz responses are included below.

- Drawing conclusions: There is a great threshold to be crossed between comparing and contrasting on the one hand and drawing conclusions on the other, and it is one that I may have taken too lightly, for my students were not prepared for it the first time I did this unit. They were able to respond to contrast, but to my disappointment they were not prepared to interpret the significance of those contrasts. I needed to create questions that helped the students come to a deeper level of understanding. For example, I asked the class what question the Beast asks, again and again, in the movie ("Do you love me?") and in the book ("Will you marry me?"). This allowed us to talk about such oppositions as *long term* versus *short term* and *action* versus *feeling*.

However, a dynamic learning activity allows for an unforeseen response. In one class, I discovered that the students' favorable impression of the movie

---

Quiz Responses

1. (In the movie, the horse returns without the father. In the text), *father promises the beast that he would come back.*

2. (In the movie, the horse returns without the father. In the text), *father came back.*

3. (In the movie, the horse returns without the father. In the text), *Beauty's father come back home, but bring a lot sad, because he need to give one of his daughters to the Beast.*

4. (In the movie, the father is imprisoned by the Beast for just being on his property. In the text), *the father is imprisoned for try to cut a rose.*

5. (In the movie, Beauty first sees the prince in a forbidden wing of the house. In the text), *Beauty meet the prince in a dream, and next in a portrait.*

6. (In the movie, we learn the Beast is a man early in the story. In the text), *beauty dream a handsome prince.*

7. (In the movie, the Beast has a goofy smile and terrible table manners. In the text), *in the book he is very ugly too, but his very gentle.*

8. (In the movie, Beauty learns about the place she is away from by looking in a special mirror. In the text), *she learns by dreams.*

was not always simply a matter of being unthinking or uncritical. Some students managed to come up with persuasive reasons for their preferences: "The movie changes a lot of the book . . . I think to make the story more commercial and attractive to adults of all ages." ". . . add more person like Gaston to show him like 'the villain-hero' and his follower to add more comedy to the film." "Disney movie makes the movie more fun and make kids interesting and shows the danger of world like Gaston and villagers." I might disagree about the effects of certain changes, but I could not argue with the premise that the film was simply trying to appeal by being enjoyable.

> Maybe teachers give too little time to true critical thinking. Too often, it becomes interpreting data—working with words in a way that allows for only one possible outcome, such as taking a line graph and asking the students to put it into sentence format or taking a primary document, such as a journal, and asking the students, for example, to "describe some of the hardships of the Santa Fe trail."

- Finding deeper meaning: Perhaps it is not so surprising that students are good at noticing contrasts but cannot take the next step, making inferences. One way to encourage more thoughtfulness may be to regularly and unfailingly ask, whether the source is a primary document, a textbook, or a work of literature, questions such as "What is this source telling us? What does it want to get across? What picture is it presenting to us?" And, finally, "Does this picture square with what we already know about the subject?" I try to ask these questions right after such questions as "Tell about the strengths and weaknesses of . . ." and "Put yourself in the position of . . . ." Again, I suggest something like Aesop's fables to be a good model for such thinking as a way of shaping information into patterns and meaning.

- Preparing for writing: After experiencing a minimum of four versions of *Beauty and the Beast*, we brainstorm the components of the story: What must one have to make a version of *Beauty and the Beast*? One class came up with these components:

    1. Beauty

    2. a Beast, that is, a man who had a spell cast upon him making him appear to be a monster

    3. Beauty's father, who is in some way responsible for her predicament

    4. a palace with a garden

I ask the class to copy these notes in case they wish to write their own version.

Writing Tasks and Assessment

Having the students do a writing task is a good way to close the unit and provide an assessment. In thinking about the nature of the tasks, I want to be sure the students' options reflect the breadth of activities involved in the unit, the variety of genres they have studied, and the various writing goals I have for the students.

Of the eight principles of assessment put forward in *Scenarios for Standards-Based Assessment* (TESOL, in press), I believe three are crucial for use in this unit.

1. "Assessments draw on the social, cultural, and academic experiences of ESOL learners" (TESOL, in press). I want to be sure that the students can draw on their strengths to produce positive work. Because comparing and contrasting are important thinking and writing aspects of the unit, integrating the student's life into the assignment is a natural process. One option is for the students to write about two people they know or two places they know.

2. "Classroom assessments enable the students to demonstrate their learning in multiple ways from multiple perspectives, thus serving as learning experiences themselves" (TESOL, in press). I want the students' involvement with the project they choose to reflect the enjoyment that I believe they should experience with the unit as a whole. I therefore give them choices involving different kinds of writing, ranging from writing that imitates or approximates the story and poem forms they have been reading to writing that lends itself to personal reflection.

3. "Classroom assessments mirror the language(s) and content of instruction and instructional practices" (TESOL, in press). It is a great advantage when the students can use the style and format of language they have been studying and imitate that style for their own use. Clearly, an assessment of the value of a poem will employ a very different set of language strategies than will an exposition showing comparison and contrast.

> ### *Goal 3, Standard 1*   To use English in socially and culturally appropriate ways: Students will use appropriate language variety, register, and genre according to audience, purpose and setting.
>
> #### *Descriptors*
> - responding to and using idioms appropriately
> - responding to and using slang appropriately
> - using a variety of writing styles appropriate for different audiences, purposes, and settings
>
> #### *Progress Indicators*
> - write a dialogue incorporating idioms or slang
> - use idiomatic speech appropriately
> - recognize irony, sarcasm, and humor in a variety of contexts

PROCEDURE

- Choosing writing tasks: In the culminating assignment, students choose two of the following three writing tasks:

  1. Write your own version of *Beauty and the Beast.* Be as free as possible as long as you include the necessary components.

2. Write a poem (or story) with a metaphor.

3. Compare two things, noting similarities and differences (e.g., yourself now and yourself 5 years ago; two family members; two cities where you used to live, or a city in your native country and the city you live in now).

• Prompting writing through literature and corresponding movies: There are many possibilities for prompting a wide range of writing. The students could take any book that has been adapted into film (e.g., *Matilda,* Dahl, 1988; *Tuck Everlasting,* Babbitt, 1976; or, on a different level, *To Kill a Mockingbird,* Lee, 1960) and follow the pattern of activities that they have completed for the "Beauty and the Beast" unit. The students can write a quiz based on contrast, with sentences beginning with a statement about the story in one genre, leaving the second part to be filled in (see p. 45).

• Prompting cause, comparison, and contrast through movies: A number of films of the 1980s and 1990s used fantasy to consider reality as a series of options that are contingent upon cause. This approach offers great possibilities for visualizing comparison and contrast, because the causes for differences are found in the story itself rather than in a conclusion to be drawn. For example, how and why is Marty McFly's family at the end of *Back to the Future* (Gale, Canton, & Zemeckis, 1985) different from the same family at the beginning of the film? Why and how is the town at the end of *Jumanji* (Kroopf, Tetler, & Johnston, 1996) different from the same town at the beginning? How is Phil Connors a different person at the end of *Groundhog Day* (Albert, Ramis, & Ramis, 1993)? These stories have some character development, but in addition they have stark contrasts based on changing circumstances that allow a writer to note substantial differences and at the same time explore the effects of human action.

• Encouraging different kinds of writing: Assignments can be based on poems and stories with different requirements and degrees of formality. One example is a true story involving someone who had to go somewhere he or she did not want to go because they cared about another person; another is a poem addressing the main character of a story by name and written in the vocative mood ("Dearest Beauty, have no fear . . .," see p. 40), thus allowing for the investigation of the formal and structural qualities of language in a literary context.

• Creating the final product: Together we choose some of the writing and put together a book, using a laminator and a binding machine. Most of the writing excerpts in this unit are from such a book, entitled *What Is & What If.* As the students choose their piece of writing, I encourage them to look for writing that allows the reader to visualize what the writer was seeing.

Student Work

Variations

Shanky's Variation

Once there was a girl called Beauty and she lived in a castle in the woods. She was changed into a horrible beast. There was a boy living in the woods, and he got changed into a girl. Beauty loved flowers and she had a big maze in the middle of the garden. The boy that got changed into a girl rode through the maze in the garden. When she was about to go back, the beast jumped out, the girl jumped up in the air, and fell on the ground. The beast said, "Why are you in my garden?" The girl said, "I am just looking at the flowers." "You will die," said the beast. Right after that, the beast's father said, "Leave the girl alone and go in your room." Then they both fell in love. After that, they both turned into themselves.

—Shanky Verma

Fortunato's Variation

Beauty and the Beast

Once upon a time, there was a girl called Beast, and she lived in an old house, in which the roof was falling apart, and a piece was falling on her father's head. His head was broken in half. One piece was of head was falling on the floor and a piece was stuck on his body. After all this mess, her father invented a machine to cut wood. He tried the machine, and the machine blew up. He made another one and he sold it. In the road he was lost, so he ran and some wolf attacked him, and he ran into a castle and got in. When he got in, some silly and crazy people served him, and Beauty came and scared him, and put him in cages with pigs and cows, and his daughter came and saved him, but when his daughter saw him she went away from her father because there was a room so stinky. The Beast and Beauty then met and fell in love, and her father died in that room with the stink of the animals.

—Fortunato Parlato

Comparisons

Jessica's Comparison

I have two sisters, they have a few things in common, but they are very different people.

Kimberly is tall, she has brown hair and brown eyes, she is 12 years old. Christina is small with blond hair and blue eyes, and she is 11. They are very different in their personalities. Christina is more outgoing, she makes friends really quickly, but Kimberly tries sports, she gives up too fast, Kimberly tries more, she tries to be like me all the time, but too picky with her food, Chris eats almost everything. My older sister hates to wear dresses, but Christina loves it. Christina loves soccer, just like me, but Kim doesn't.

My younger sister eats breakfast in the morning, the other doesn't. Kimberly gets up quickly in the morning, but Christina needs an hour. They are really different, but they also have some things in common. They both play Baseball and their rooms are always messy. Chris and Kim have the same best friend which I can't understand.

Both of them borrow my clothes all the time. They like the same music and Boy Groups. One big thing they have in common is: laziness, they hate to fold clothes and clean their rooms. Kim & Chris love rainbow sprinkles on their ice cream. They know how to use the computer. In school they have the same grades, and one big thing that everybody has in common and hates: HOMEWORK.

—Jessica Dietl

Tina's Comparison

About Vietnam

In Vietnam I lived in the city, but I like the village better because the village is a beautiful place. There are so many things to remember. In the village around 5–5:30 in the morning, the rooster crows, everyone in the village wakes up ready to go to the rice field. They stay in the morning till dawn, they work hard but they feel comfortable about it. In the village, some people are poor and some of them are rich.

Around 8 in the morning, some of the people sell stuff on the street. They sell fish, meats, herbs, salads, etc. People buy it for the day. Sometimes people go to a big market, but it takes 30–45 minutes to get there. In the afternoon, after they eat lunch, they take a nap and go to the rice field to work again. In the evening around 9–9:30 the sun sets.

Pretend you're standing in the middle of the rice field. When the sun goes down, the sky has so many colors, like orange, red, purple and pink. The sun is big and red. The wind blows the rice field like a wave, and you stand far away, you can see some of the people using oil lamps. Around their house are coconut trees and some of the kids sit on the ox's back and play flute. What a romantic place. In front of you the sun sets, all around you are rice fields, you can hear the sound of the flute and the wind is lifting your hair up. At night, the moon is big and bright. When I look up in the sky, it has many stars. Some of the people live next to the rice field. At night the frog croaks and some people go outside and play blindman. When they get tired, they go home to bed and ready for tomorrow.

In the city it is a little different from the village because the village is quiet but the city is noisy. The city has so many motorcycles, people who live there are all rich, not like in the village. In Vietnam, I lived next to the beach, and I went there every evening. Sometimes I watched the sun set. When the sun went down, I could see the water reflected. I wish some day that I would go back to my country and I'll do the same thing that I did as a child.

—Tina Nguyen

Metaphors and Identities

Ivna's Metaphor

even know I remember that my heart remembers the time you were with me and you loved me more than we could see i still remember that our love is like a forest with rose like our love so sweet.

—Ivna Aragao

Arijana's Identity

I am a girl who likes to think a lot
I am a girl who loves to wonder
I am a girl that has lots of dreams
I am a girl that loves her dreams

I pretend that I don't dream that much
I pretend that I don't wonder a lot
I pretend that I don't have lots of dreams
I pretend that I don't love my dreams

I know that I like to think a lot
I know that I like to wonder a lot
I know that I have lots of dreams
I know that I love my dreams and my wonders!

—Arijana Kezo

RESOURCES AND REFERENCES

Classroom Resources

Babbitt, N. (1976). *Tuck everlasting*. New York: Bantam Books.

Dahl, R. (1988). *Matilda*. New York: Puffin.

Gerstein, M. (1989). *Beauty and the beast*. New York: E. P. Dutton.
  The book's illustrations, along with the text, tell the story in sharp, quick strokes.

Lang, A. (1965). *The blue fairy book*. New York: Dover. (Original work published 1899)
  This book contains the classic version of "Beauty and the Beast," in Victorian prose.

Lawrence, J. (1997). *Aesop's fables*. Seattle: University of Washington Press.
  I find this a useful edition, with direct, colloquial speech.

Lee, H. (1960). *To kill a mockingbird*. New York: Lippincott.

Salter, S. (1992). *Aesop's fables*. San Diego: Harcourt Brace Jovanovich.

Sawyer, R. (1970). *The way of the storyteller*. New York: Penguin Books.

Videos

Albert, T., Ramis, H. (Producers), & Ramis, H. (Director). (1993). *Groundhog day* [Video]. (Available from Columbia Tri Star Home Video, 3400 Riverside Dr., Burbank, CA 91505)

Ashman, H., Hahn, D. (Producers), Truesdale, G., & Wise, K. (Directors). (1991). *Beauty and the beast* [Video]. (Available from Buena Vista, Dept. CS, Burbank, CA 91521)

Gale, B., Canton, N. (Producers), & Zemeckis, R. (Director). (1985). *Back to the future* [Video]. (Available from MCA Home Video, 70 Universal City Plaza, Universal City, CA 91608)

Green, J. (Producer), & Gerstein, M. (Director). (1992). *Beauty and the beast* [Video]. (Available from Lightyear Video, Lightyear Entertainment, Empire State Building, New York, NY 10118)

Kroopf, S., Tetler, W. (Producers), & Johnston, J. (Director). (1996). *Jumanji* [Video]. (Available from Tri Star, 10202 West Washington Blvd., Culver City, CA 90232-3195)

Terry, B., Fuchs, F. (Producers), & Vadim, R. (Director). (1984). *Beauty and the beast* [Video]. (Available from CBS/Fox Video, Industrial Park Drive, Farmington Hills, MI 48335)

Teacher References

Barton, B., & Booth, D. (1990). *Stories in the classroom.* Portsmouth, NH: Heinemann.
Of full-time professional storytellers, Barton, a Canadian, is among the most knowledgeable about education. This book emphasizes the importance of listening to children tell their stories.

Bettelheim, B. (1977). *The uses of enchantment.* New York: Vintage Books.
No other book that I know of so vividly demonstrates how stories work as metaphor.

Bruner, J. (1966). *Toward a theory of instruction.* New York: Norton.
Bruner comes from a background of mathematics and cognitive theory. His observations on children's need for a storehouse of images in order to make sense of the world are remarkable in their relevance to storytelling.

Egan, K. (1986). *Teaching as storytelling.* Chicago: University of Chicago Press.
As the title indicates, this book is not so much about how teachers can do storytelling as about how they already do.

Mooney, B., & Holt, D. (1996). *The storyteller's guide.* Little Rock, AR: August House.
This is an essential resource for the contemporary beginning or practiced storyteller. It includes how to choose and tell stories, build storytelling programs, create opportunities for tellings, deal with copyright, and so forth, all expressed anecdotally in the words of the top storytellers working today.

Sawyer, R. (1970). *The way of the storyteller.* New York: Penguin Books. (Original work published 1942)
Sawyer makes the connection between books and telling better than anyone. In this book she does not so much tell people how to tell stories as awaken the love and belief people already have for them. Besides sharing an incredibly rich sense of cultural resources, she includes 11 of the stories she told, several of which are classics that beg to be retold. This book moved me to become a storyteller.

Shedlock, M. (1951). *The art of the storyteller.* New York: Dover.
Shedlock, who died in 1935, led the way in reviving storytelling as an art that can introduce children to literature.

Stafford, W. (1978). *Writing the Australian crawl.* Ann Arbor: The University of Michigan Press.

TESOL. (1997). *ESL standards for pre-K–12 students.* Alexandria, VA: Author.

TESOL. (in press). *Scenarios for ESL standards-based assessment.* Alexandria, VA: Author.

UNIT 3
The Scientific Method and Experimental Design

CYNTHIA LEIGH ROSS

Introduction

Ray, a beginning-level English learner, bounded into our ESL room, which for its other life as a biology classroom was lined with skulls, posters illustrating biological structures and processes, and aquariums containing snakes, turtles, an iguana, some rodents, and a prize collection of Madagascar hissing cockroaches. He glanced at the overhead transparency, which the biology teacher had left behind, then examined it more closely.

"What is that?" he demanded, eyeing the chart of 23 pairs of nearly indistinguishable Xs.

"That's a karyotype, a chart that shows human chromosomes. Chromosomes are the directions for making humans and human cells. Every normal human has 23 pairs just like those," I answered. I knew from experience that Ray's enthusiasm for learning—any subject, any time—would require a thorough explanation, which I feared I was not prepared to give. Although I had spent the year in the biology class as a resource teacher, my grip on this particular branch of knowledge might not be firm enough to withstand the coming storm of questions. Psychically willing the biology teacher to return to the room and bail me out, I braced myself.

"Kar-y-o-type. Karyotype. I learned that 2 years ago in Korea." Pleased with himself, Ray sat down, opened his notebook, and began

Context

Grade levels: 9th–11th grades

English proficiency levels: Beginning–low intermediate

Native languages of students: Spanish, Korean, Vietnamese, Farsi, Chinese

Focus of instruction: Science/ESL

Type of class: Sheltered content, team-taught with science teacher

Length of unit: 2 weeks

sketching what I hoped was an illustration for his group's presentation on the novel Dracula. I was relieved, but a minute later he sprang back to my desk with an elaborate diagram that included a collection of partially unzipped zippers with teeth labeled A, C, G, and T.

"There is something I forgot, Ms. Ross. Can you explain what is different between tRNA and mRNA?"

Unit Overview

Science for Secondary ESOL Students

When I learned that I would be team-teaching Science Concepts, I was delighted—pleased to have the challenge of doing something that was new and different for me, happy to be reaching out into a new content area and department, and eager to teach science in an ESL context. Close on the heels of that elation, however, came intimidation and something that very closely resembled panic. I am no scientist—and where was I to start?

Science Concepts is designed to provide beginning-level ESOL students with basic scientific concepts and vocabulary that they will need as a foundation for future main-stream science classes, especially life sciences. My Concepts team-teacher and I knew this would not be easy. In our district and especially in our school, these students often come from a wide range of academic experiences, from students who have had limited or interrupted education to those who are on grade level in their native languages, sometimes beyond U.S. students of the same age. At one end of the spectrum, students may have difficulty understanding the conceptual difference between *living* and *nonliving*. Why is fire not a living thing, if it grows, moves, breathes, and eats? At the other end, of course, are students like Ray, who can dance rings around his ESL teacher scientifically.

My Concepts team-teacher, the same biology teacher with whom I had worked as a resource, had asked to teach Concepts for the same reason I had—for the challenge of expanding his horizons beyond his usual class assignments. We both looked forward to stretching ourselves in order to better prepare our students for their future education. But again—how were we to get started?

We already knew how to prepare students for biology, which would be their first mainstream science class, so we also examined the curricula for physics, chemistry, and earth science. In addition to looking at science curricula, we also

- spoke with science and ESL teachers who had taught Concepts in the past

- consulted with other ESL, science, and health/physical education (PE) staff to determine where ESOL students tended to struggle in mainstream science and health classes

- informally asked advanced-level ESOL students about their mainstream science classes and solicited their advice about Concepts topics

- last but certainly not least, examined the Virginia science standards (Commonwealth of Virginia Board of Education, 1995) as well as *ESL Standards for Pre-K–12 Students* (TESOL, 1997).

Unit Goals

This unit is designed to introduce in English some basic ideas that are the foundation for any science course: the scientific method and experimental design. Some students have already learned these approaches in their first languages and thus are primarily transferring that knowledge into English, but other students are learning the concepts for the first time. For all students, application of the scientific method and experimental design requires the exercise of both written and oral language in social and academic registers.

To supplement class activities, we ask the students to keep learning logs or journals throughout the year to allow them to work through concepts on their own terms. Throughout this description of the unit, I have included possible journal prompts (at several levels) with other suggestions. These prompts can also be used as discussion questions, for paired writing-response activities, for traditional graded writing assignments, and so forth.

In addition, we include an activity to develop skills in observation and description. We also integrate some mathematical exercises and vocabulary based on measurement (linear, mass, volume, temperature, and time) as part of data collection and interpretation. Measurement exercises focus on the metric system, the method preferred in science, although we do include some English measurements to ensure that the students have some knowledge of the system used most widely in the United States.

The course has the following goals. Students will

- understand basic scientific concepts and vocabulary in life and physical sciences in preparation for further study

- apply the principles of scientific investigation to decision making in their lives outside school

- demonstrate understanding of the relevance of science to historical and current events locally and globally

- develop and adapt strategies for learning science

- develop and adapt strategies for recording and locating information through note-taking, notebook organization, research in print and electronic media, reading strategies, and other means

- use the four language skills and both social and academic registers in scientific investigation and communication

The unit goals are as follows. Students will

- apply the steps of the scientific method to investigate a problem and determine possible solutions

- recognize the link between scientific method as theory and experimental design as application

- design an experiment, identifying independent and dependent variables, constants, and controls, in order to test a hypothesis

- use both metric and English forms of linear, mass, volume, and temperature measurement in the collection of quantitative data

- recognize the importance of careful observation and description in obtaining and recording qualitative data

- use the language of science in solving problems

- increase their knowledge of English grammar and vocabulary through language activities integrated into the study of the scientific method and experimental design

Because the unit is intended to establish basic ideas about the nature and means of scientific inquiry, I present it as early as possible in the school year, after the class has completed such introductory and administrative work as lab rules, safety issues, and notebook organization.

The unit overview gives a visual representation of the unit.

The Class

The class comprised 25 beginning-level ESOL students. Our school divides beginning-level students into three groups, of which the first two would be enrolled in the Concepts course:

1. *low beginning students (Low A),* who have recently come to the United States but may have learned some English in formal or informal contexts before their arrival. They have three periods of ESL; many of them will also be enrolled in either an individualized math course taught by an ESL teacher or an algebra course assisted by an ESL resource teacher. PE and art classes may be their only mainstream classes.

2. *high beginning students (High A),* who may have been in the country for a year or more or have had some formal English instruction in the past. They have three ESL classes and are often mainstreamed in math, PE, art, or elective courses.

3. *literacy students (LA level),* who have very low skills in English and may have had limited or interrupted education in their first language. They have four class periods of ESL and may be enrolled in the individualized math course taught by an ESL teacher; PE and fine or performing arts classes may be their only mainstream classes. (These students would not be enrolled in Concepts.)

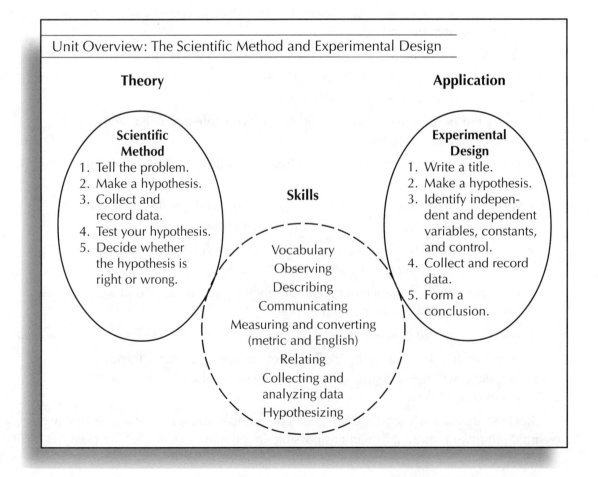

A majority of the students enrolled in Concepts are classified as High A. Many of the students have studied English in their native countries; they often have fairly strong skills in written language but weaker skills in speaking and listening. Others have been in the United States for several years and show strong speaking and listening skills but have not achieved the same level in reading and writing. The students' science backgrounds vary as well; some have strong science backgrounds, but others have had little formal education in science.

When I first taught the course, I was fortunate in that I had every Concepts student for one to two periods of ESL language as well. This meant I was able to complement the science work with language minilessons during regular ESL class time when necessary, integrating science and language instruction more smoothly.

Standards

In planning a unit, I tend to begin by sketching out content, activities, and themes, and then I tie those ideas to more concrete standards. Plans may change during the course of a unit according to the students' interest and need, but periodically I step back and look at the big picture to ensure that the class is still moving in the intended direction, developing targeted skills in a balanced fashion.

In this case, my team-teacher and I had two sets of standards to work with, science and ESL. A review of *Science Standards of Learning for Virginia Public Schools* (Commonwealth of Virginia Board of Education, 1995) revealed a recurring emphasis from the very beginning on investigation and understanding. The use of *investigate* and *understand* was intended to encourage educators to see the standards as a broad range of teaching objectives rather than as limited observable behaviors. To assist with interpretation of the standards, the document enlarges upon the terms as shown in the "Inquiry Skills and Knowledge Application Chart."

Inquiry Skills and Knowledge Application Chart

Investigation Inquiry Skills	**Understanding** Levels of Knowledge Application
• observing • classifying and sequencing • communicating • measuring • predicting • hypothesizing • inferring • defining, controlling, and manipulating variables • designing, constructing, and interpreting models • interpreting, analyzing, and evaluating data	• recalling and recognizing important information • explaining and relating • applying knowledge to new problems • analyzing underlying details and patterns • synthesizing new ideas from known facts and principles • judging accuracy, precision, consistency, or effectiveness

Adapted from Commonwealth of Virginia Board of Education (1995).

Although I thought at first the science standards might be intimidating, they strengthened my belief that science can be an exciting framework through which to teach language. The ESL standards can easily and organically be integrated into objectives such as those described on page 57. In addition, science encourages, indeed requires, the teacher to use a wealth of strategies and resources, including hands-on experiments and inquiries, demonstrations, computer labs and simulations, living organisms, and all manner of models and realia to bring the subject to life. In this case, we planned to bring language and science to life together.

Activities

The unit necessarily begins with a pretest to assess how much science the students know. The first time I taught the course, I already knew a number of the students from the previous year, and I had a great deal of data on most of those who were new to me; however, most of that information was related to language, and we had little information on the students' science backgrounds. The pretest, which requires a full class period for administration and review, covers measurement, basic mathematical skills, estimation, and interpretation of charts and graphs.

Science and the Scientific Method

Because this first activity is the introduction to an entire year of science study, we want to establish a common understanding of just what science is. This introductory activity requires two to three class periods.

Goal 2, Standard 2 **To use English to achieve academically in all content areas: Students will use English to obtain, process, construct, and provide subject matter information in spoken and written form.**

Descriptors

- persuading, arguing, negotiating, evaluating, and justifying
- listening to, speaking, reading, and writing about subject matter information
- gathering information orally and in writing
- retelling information
- selecting, connecting, and explaining information
- representing information visually and interpreting information presented visually

Progress Indicators

- compare and classify information using technical vocabulary
- work with peers to establish and negotiate meaning in response to a discussion question
- select relevant material to record in writing or as a poster
- present results of discussion to large group
- explain concepts in response to peer or teacher questions

PROCEDURE

- Introduction: We ask the students, "What is science?" We invite students at every level to contribute, whether they choose simply to translate the word into their language or offer a more detailed definition. We write all contributions on the board or on an overhead transparency for reference. We emphasize the nature of science as problem solving. The result might look like this:

  Science is

  knowledge of organized facts and laws

  humans creating things to make life more comfortable

  study of nature through observation and experiments

  natural ideas you can use to make or explain things

- Group work: Next, we divide the students into four heterogeneous groups. Although it is early in the year and we have not yet had time to get a feel for each individual student, we try to mix them by personality types as well as by English proficiency and native language. We do not want all the shy students in one group any more than we want all the Spanish speakers together. We also try to ensure that each group includes at least one student with strong oral skills and one with strong skills in written language, so that each group can select a presenter and a recorder.

- Problem solving: Each group is given a problem and the task of describing it and outlining the steps one might take in solving that problem. We model the procedure for them and discuss it briefly:

  Step 1. Say what is wrong: "My locker won't open today, but I got it open last week."

  Step 2. Think about why this could happen: "Maybe I don't remember the combination correctly."

  Step 3. Think about a solution: "I can check the combination to be sure it's right."

  Step 4. Try your solution: "Go to the office and check your locker combination."

  Step 5. Solve the problem: "Try to open your locker with the right combination. Does it open? If it does, great! If not, what can you do?" (Make sure that it is the right locker; check to make sure that you turn the dial in the correct direction; ask a custodian to see if it is broken.)

- Presentation of the scientific method: Once the students have had time to complete and present their problem-solution procedures, we continue the discussion by presenting the scientific method, explaining that this is how scientists solve science problems:

  Step 1. State the problem.

  Step 2. Make a hypothesis.

  Step 3. Collect and record data.

  Step 4. Use the data to check the hypothesis.

  Step 5. Form a conclusion (decide if your hypothesis was right or wrong).

Next, we review the method step by step. Enlarging upon each step, we pay special attention to data collection, asking questions such as, "What kind of data would you need to solve a certain problem?" "How can you measure the data?" "Can all data be measured?" We emphasize the importance of clear, accurate record keeping and remind the students of the care they have taken in setting up their notebooks the previous week. We then ask them, in pairs, to write another example for the scientific method, this time including the kinds of data that might be necessary to test the hypothesis. This leads us into the next activity, Measurement (p. 63).

SUGGESTIONS, ALTERNATIVES, AND ASSESSMENT

We ask the students to organize their notebooks fairly simply, by unit, rather than placing homework, quizzes and tests, notes, and journal entries in separate sections. The students keep materials in chronological order. Once or twice a unit we give a "notebook quiz": We hand out a checklist of required items 2 days in advance and then collect the notebooks to check for completeness. This helps the students understand the importance of organization and record keeping.

Vocabulary can include *science, method, problem, hypothesis, research, data, test, conclusion, analyze, record, solution.* I generally use fairly short vocabulary lists because, rather than feeding the students dictionary or prefabricated definitions, I like to work with the students to negotiate a succinct but correct definition that we then use throughout the unit. The words are then theirs as much as they are mine, and the language of the definitions can be tailored to the needs of the students. This negotiation is not always possible, but I find it gets the students talking and thinking about meanings and shades of meaning.

The students can be challenged with additional vocabulary work. A variety of crossword puzzles or other word games can reinforce understanding of the terms; the students can also be asked to look up dictionary definitions or find related words or synonyms. They might also study parts of speech with those words that are both nouns and verbs (*research, test, record*) or, for the more advanced students, through suffixes that change meaning or part of speech (*science/scientist, conclusion/conclude, analysis/ analyze, hypothesis/hypothesize*).

Some students can create posters to illustrate the method. These we put up on the walls for future reference. The posters benefit not only the Concepts class but also the biology classes that meet in the same classroom. The information can also be presented as a flowchart or other graphic organizer. Teachers willing to dedicate extra instructional time can have the students write and produce a short video explaining the scientific method.

Learning log prompts for this activity might include the following:

- A scientist uses the scientific method to solve problems. Who else can use the scientific method to solve problems? Can a teacher? A student? A mechanic? A doctor? A computer programmer? An artist?

- Pretend your friend asks you what you study in Concepts. Explain the scientific method for your friend.

- Why do you think we study the scientific method?

- Can you use the scientific method in your life? How?

These activities can be used to assess the students' understanding of the nature of science.

Sample Student Learning Log Response

I think our life is science. Not only in our science class, but also farming, fishing, etc. For example, we are farmed by machine, combain, plane etc.

Measurement

In this activity, we discuss and practice various means of measuring data. We allow two to three class periods to review the metric system (particularly unit conversions using multiples of 10) as well as the English system, and to complete the measurement activity.

Goal 2, Standard 3   **To use English to achieve academically in all content areas: Students will use appropriate learning strategies to construct and apply academic knowledge.**

Descriptors

- focusing attention selectively
- applying basic reading comprehension skills such as skimming, scanning, previewing, and reviewing text
- taking notes to record important information and aid one's own learning
- actively connecting new information to information previously learned

Progress Indicators

- use measurement vocabulary
- select and convert between metric or English system measurements, using notes as reference
- question and defend data
- explain rationale for answers

PROCEDURE

- Introduction: We introduce measurement using the "Measurement Transparency" (pp. 64–65) and a corresponding handout on the metric and English systems. The handout has blanks for students to fill in key pieces— metric prefixes, conversion factors, and so forth—as we go over the information on the overhead projector.
- Measurement: After the introduction, student pairs move through the classroom measuring specimens, furniture, teachers, and so forth, and recording their measurements on the worksheet shown on page 66. We require them to show units of measurement, perform one conversion between the two systems, and identify the systems they use. We include

---

Measurement Transparency

Metric System

The metric system is based on 10s. These are the basic units in the metric system:

Unit	Measures
meter (m)	length
gram (g)	mass
liter (l)	volume
degrees Celsius (°C)	temperature

The metric system uses prefixes. The prefixes tell you *how many* or *what part* of the basic unit. (Note: You never use a prefix for temperature.) The prefixes are listed below from smallest to largest.

Prefix	milli	centi	deci	—	deka	hecto	kilo
Abbreviation	m	c	d	—	dk	h	k
Multiply by	.001	.01	.1	1	10	100	1,000

Put the prefix on the front of the basic unit word: *centi*meter, *kilo*gram, *milli*liter.

Say you need 3 meters of wood to build bookshelves. How many centimeters of wood is that?

Three meters equals how many
centimeters times .01? → $3\ m = X\ cm \times .01\ m/cm$

Three meters divided by .01 equals
how many centimeters? → $3\ m/.01\ m = X\ cm$

Three divided by .01 equals 300. → $300 = X$

Three meters equals 300 centimeters. → $3\ m = 300\ cm$

You have 10 kg of sugar. Your favorite cake recipe takes 500 g of sugar. How many cakes can you make for a party?

Divide 10 kilograms by 500 grams
for every cake. → $10\ kg/500\ g$

Oops! Convert kilograms to grams.

10 kilograms times 1,000 is
10,000 grams. → $10\ kg \times 1,000 = 10,000\ g$

10,000 grams divided by
500 grams is 20 cakes. → $10,000\ g/500\ g = 20$ cakes

continued on p. 65

---

several blanks to allow the students to select distinctive items for measurement. To foster a sense of the class as a social entity as well as to encourage social use of language, we encourage the students to be creative or even silly in their selections (e.g., the height of Billie [the class skeleton], the length of the boa constrictor, the weight of the hamster, the volume of a

Measurement Transparency, *continued*

English System

The English system is common in the United States. It does not use the tens system.

Length				*Metric Units*
1 inch (in.)	=		=	2.54 cm
1 foot (ft)	=	12 in.	=	.305 m
1 yard (yd)	=	3 ft	=	.914 m
1 mile (mi)	=	5,280 ft	=	1.609 km

Weight				
1 ounce (oz)	=		=	28.375 g
1 pound (lb)	=	16 oz	=	.454 kg
1 ton	=	2,000 lb	=	907.185 kg

Volume				
1 fluid ounce (fl oz)	=		=	29.574 ml
1 cup (c)	=	8 oz	=	.237 l
1 pint (pt)	=	2 c	=	.474 l
1 quart (qt)	=	2 pt	=	.948 l
1 gallon (gal)	=	4 qt	=	3.792 l

Temperature

Temperature is different. You cannot just multiply once; you have to use this formula:

$$\text{(temperature in degrees Fahrenheit} - 32)/1.8 = \text{temperature in degrees Celsius}$$

So, to convert 68°F to Celsius:

$$(68°F - 32)/1.8 = 36/1.8 = 20°C$$

To convert Celsius to Fahrenheit, use this formula:

$$\text{(temperature in degrees Celsius} \times 1.8) + 32 = \text{temperature in degrees Fahrenheit}$$

$$(100°C \times 1.8) + 32 = 180 + 32 = 212°F$$

teacher's ever-present coffee cup). When the activity is complete, we ask student pairs to briefly compare results before going over the answers with the whole group.

- Conversions: Knowing that conversions sometimes can be a problem, we challenge the class to convert measurements selected at random from the activity, both within the metric system and between the English and metric systems. The first student to produce the correct answer explains his or her reasoning to the class.

Measurement Worksheet

With your partner, measure each of the things. Use two different units. Convert the units by multiplying or dividing. Follow the example.
(M = metric and E = English)

Example: Ms. Ross (height)   63 inches E   =   1.6 meters M

1. bone (length)   _____   =   _____
2. desk (height)   _____   =   _____
3. flower (width)   _____   =   _____
4. Mr. Dux's shoe (length)   _____   =   _____
5. door (width)   _____   =   _____
6. quarter (mass)   _____   =   _____
7. nut (mass)   _____   =   _____
8. classroom (temperature)   _____   =   _____
9. water (temperature)   _____   =   _____
10. soda can (volume)   _____   =   _____

Now choose five more things in the classroom to measure. Use three different units.

1. _____   _____   =   _____   =   _____
2. _____   _____   =   _____   =   _____
3. _____   _____   =   _____   =   _____
4. _____   _____   =   _____   =   _____
5. _____   _____   =   _____   =   _____

SUGGESTIONS, ALTERNATIVES, AND ASSESSMENT

Vocabulary may include *measure, metric, English (Imperial), system, unit, temperature, linear, long, length, mass, weigh, weight, volume, cubic, convert/conversion.*

The measurement transparency (pp. 64–65) can be used in a variety of ways:

- Distribute a copy to the students.
- Replace some of the text with blanks, encouraging the students to take notes without overwhelming them with the quantity of information presented.
- Simply display the transparency, and direct the students to take notes on a blank piece of notebook paper.

This activity can also be complemented by language minilessons on

- adjectives such as *heavy, light, hot, warm, cool, cold, long, tall, short, wide, narrow*
- comparatives and superlatives

> **Sample Student Learning Log Responses**
>
> I like metric system much better. The small reason is I used metric system in Korea So It's easy to me. And large reason is that world is becoming smaller, then of course we must unify the unit.
>
> I think Americans should know both way, not just one system. By the way in most of countries they use metric system. So I think learn both way are better.

- interrogative structures such as *how much, how many,* and *how long/hot/ heavy*
- count and noncount nouns in the context of measurement
- structures such as *the table is 1.5 meters long, he weighs 120 pounds,* and *the temperature of the water is 57 degrees Celsius.*

Learning log prompts for this activity might include

- In your country, do you use the metric system or the English system to measure things?
- Do you like the metric or English system better? Why?
- Americans usually use the English system instead of the metric system. Do you think Americans should use the metric system more? Why or why not?
- Scientists usually use the metric system. Can you explain why?

We assess understanding of the systems of measurement and conversions on an ongoing basis through measurement activities and through later activities requiring data collection. Teachers may also wish to design an activity using the World Wide Web site published by participants in the ThinkQuest Junior program (ThinkQuest Junior Team 3804, 1998). This site contains useful information on measurement, English and metric, written at an upper elementary level. It also includes a practice activity and simple conversion programs. The students could explore and evaluate the site and then enter their comments or suggestions in the guest book.

Observation and Description

In this activity, student teams of four use both quantitative (measurement) and qualitative data to identify an individual specimen from among a group of four items (labeled A, B, C, and D) found at their table.

This one-period activity makes the students more aware of the need for precise observation and description while affording them the chance to exercise and build descriptive vocabulary as well as practice measuring.

Procedure

- The problem: The students arrive in class to find small dishes containing four seemingly identical specimens placed at numbered stations around the room: worms, crickets, guppies, shells, lima beans, peanuts, and flowers. Each item or organism within a set is identified as A, B, C, or D.

Goal 2, Standard 2   To use English to achieve academically in all content areas: Students will use English to obtain, process, construct, and provide subject matter information in spoken and written form.

Descriptors

- comparing and contrasting information
- persuading, arguing, negotiating, evaluating, and justifying
- listening to, speaking, reading, and writing about subject matter information
- gathering information orally and in writing
- retelling information
- responding to the work of peers and others
- understanding and producing technical vocabulary according to content area

Progress Indicators

- compare and classify information using technical vocabulary
- record observations of specimens
- write clear, accurate descriptions
- interpret written descriptions

Goal 3, Standard 1   To use English in socially and culturally appropriate ways: Students will use the appropriate language variety, register, and genre according to audience, purpose, and setting.

Descriptors

- using the appropriate degree of formality with different audiences and settings
- using a variety of writing styles appropriate for different audiences, purposes, and settings

Progress Indicators

- provide information and feedback to peers, orally and in writing
- use appropriate language in interacting with group members, recording observations for classmates, and writing in journal

- Description and identification: We divide the students into teams of four and assign each team to start at one of the stations. Each team chooses one specimen from the set to observe and writes a detailed description of that specimen on the card at that station, without identifying the specimen by

```
Sample Specimen Card

From a card describing a worm:
        length: 11–15 cm (It stretch long and short)
        dark        ➔        lighter
        medium size

From a card describing a shell:
        You feel that thing hard and soft so it is so easy to break.
        It has some spots inside also has a big hole, some form are curly.
        It is the color white, brown yellow and orange
        it is 7 cm.
```

letter. After 5 minutes, the teams rotate to the next station, read the index card, and attempt to identify the specimen described. Each team comes to consensus, writes the letter of the specimen on the worksheet, and rotates to the next station. When the activity is finished, the class reviews the correct answers.

SUGGESTIONS, ALTERNATIVES, AND ASSESSMENT

Useful vocabulary for this activity includes *specimen, describe/description, observe/ observation, quantitative,* and *qualitative.*

Class discussion or journal entries can focus on the following questions:

- Was this easy or hard? Why?

- Did you write a good description? Why or why not?

- What was easier—describing or choosing? Why?

- What did you learn from this activity?

- You used lots of adjectives and numbers for this activity. Why do you think we did this activity in science class, not ESL or math?

Adequately describing their own specimens and choosing the correct specimens for other teams gives the students excellent feedback on and confidence in their ability to observe and describe. We also use student responses to discussion or journal questions to help assess the success of this activity. We always encourage the students to politely

```
Sample Description and Identification

Juan:        (examining the cricket in Dish B) What is that on B? Looks like an
             extra leg.
Mehrdad:     Only girls have it. For eggs.
Teacher:     The female uses it to lay eggs. It's called an ovipositor.
Juan:        (to team note-taker) Hey, write that! How you spell it?
```

Sample Student Learning Log Responses

We learn that no matter how much the things locks like each other they have some difrents and if we lock closer we can see that.

We learn how to descraive thing around us.

I learned if you want to describe something, you have to be careful, because if you describe something sentimentally, readers can confuse. So you should write in logical reason. Then you have to use ruler or score to measure it . . . . Because If only one person observe, then I can be subjective. But if you make a group and discuss, it'll be objective!!

---

challenge and defend data, both quantitative and qualitative, as an informal means of peer and self-assessment. The "Observing and Describing Checklist" gives the students a more concrete feel for their performance on this activity.

Observing and Describing Checklist

Name _____

Think about this activity. Choose the best response for every sentence. Did you do a good job? What did you learn? Write extra comments at the bottom.

I worked with my team to <u>observe</u> the specimens.	Yes	No	Sometimes	Don't know
I worked with my team to <u>describe</u> the specimens.	Yes	No	Sometimes	Don't know
I worked with my team to <u>write</u> about the specimens.	Yes	No	Sometimes	Don't know
I worked with my team to <u>choose</u> the specimens.	Yes	No	Sometimes	Don't know
I encouraged other students to participate.	Yes	No	Sometimes	Don't know
I was polite to other students, even if we disagreed.	Yes	No	Sometimes	Don't know
I learned or used scientific words for observing and describing specimens.	Yes	No	Sometimes	Don't know

List new scientific words here:

After this activity, the students are more attuned to the need for careful observation, description, and recording of data and, just as importantly, have practiced selecting data to be used for a particular purpose. The class is now ready to move on to experimental design.

Experimental Design

One of the goals of the unit is to help the students move from an understanding of the theory of the scientific method to its application, experimental design. We allot 2–3 days for this activity.

PROCEDURE

- Theory and application: We begin by reminding the students that the scientific method is an idea, a model for solving problems. That model can be used in real life, but scientists use it especially for solving scientific questions by designing experiments. The method is the theory; the experiment is the application. We use an adaptation of the unit overview (p. 58) to draw the parallels for the class, discussing new vocabulary as we go along. We ask the students to point out the difference between theory and application; namely, that application is concerned with the identification of variables, constants, and controls. The valid interpretation of the experiment hinges on an understanding of the relationship among these three factors.

Goal 2, Standard 2 **To use English to achieve academically in all content areas: Students will use English to obtain, process, construct, and provide subject matter information in spoken and written form.**

Descriptors

- selecting, connecting, and explaining information
- analyzing, synthesizing, and inferring from information
- hypothesizing and predicting
- formulating and asking questions
- understanding and producing technical vocabulary according to content area
- demonstrating knowledge through application in a variety of contexts

Progress Indicators

- compare and classify information using technical vocabulary
- take notes as a teacher presents information in order to summarize key concepts
- synthesize, analyze, and evaluate information
- explain change
- debate and develop ideas on process and content
- write/sketch consecutive steps in a procedure

Goal 2, Standard 3 To use English to achieve academically in all content areas: Students will use appropriate learning strategies to construct and apply academic knowledge.

Descriptors

- focusing attention selectively
- using context to construct meaning
- taking notes to record important information and aid one's own learning
- actively connecting new information to information previously learned
- evaluating one's own success in a completed learning task

Progress Indicators

- make pictures or diagrams to check comprehension
- read a narrative description of an experiment and complete an experimental design diagram
- design an experiment appropriate for testing a stated hypothesis

---

- Experimental design: We put the "Experimental Design" transparency on the overhead projector and distribute copies to the students for note-taking. On the transparency, we record vocabulary definitions as well as explanatory notes or examples, using pens of two different colors to help the students distinguish among them.

- Model experiment: We use the chicken embryo experiment as an example. "We hear that pregnant women should not drink alcohol because it can hurt the baby. We want to know what alcohol does to chicken embryos (still in the egg)."

  We get a dozen fertile eggs. We use a needle to inject a 5% alcohol solution into three eggs, 25% alcohol into three eggs, and 50% alcohol into three eggs. We put plain water into the last three eggs. We use the same amount of solution for every egg. We keep all the eggs at the same temperature for two weeks. Then we open the eggs and look at the embryos in each group.

- Mini-experiments: We distribute a selection of scenarios describing experiments, including some based on examples we used earlier for the scientific method. The students read the scenarios and work with their lab partners to write titles and hypotheses and identify independent and dependent variables, constants, and controls. Volunteers review their work on the overhead projector for the class.

- Full experimental design: Once the students are confident of their ability to identify the elements of an experiment, we put on the overhead projector an assortment of scenarios and ask pairs to choose one and design

Experimental Design

Title: *name*

"The Effect of Alcohol on Chicken Embryos"

Hypothesis: *explanation of or idea about a problem*

IF we put alcohol into chicken eggs,
THEN the alcohol will change or affect the embryos.

Independent Variables: *something in the experiment that you decide to change*

"I change the independent variable."

3 eggs	3 eggs	3 eggs	3 eggs
5% alcohol	25% alcohol	50% alcohol	plain water

Dependent Variables: *things that change because the independent variable changed; they depend on the independent variable*

The changes in the chicken embryos depend on how much alcohol we put in the eggs.

Constants: *things that don't change*

The temperature, time, needle size, and amount of solution were always the same.

Control: *the part of the experiment that you don't change; you use it for comparison with the things that you do change*

We put plain water—no alcohol—in three of the eggs. We compared the embryos that had only water to the embryos that had different amounts of alcohol.

appropriate experiments. We deliberately choose some of these problems for their relevance to the students' daily life (i.e., those that are more accessible). We take others from the students' work on the scientific method, and still others are more typically "scientific." Each pair of students briefly outlines the experiment (including the kinds of data to be collected) in writing or story board–style pictures, prepares a diagram, and explains their thinking. Here are some scenarios we have used:

Does X brand of batteries really last longer?

How many sodas can I drink before I have trouble sleeping?

Why do they put salt on icy roads?

If I spend more time studying for my weekly math quiz, will my grades go up?

Why does antifreeze keep my engine from freezing?

If I spend more time on practice, can I be a better soccer player/ musician/artist?

Is compost better for my garden than chemical fertilizer?

SUGGESTIONS, ALTERNATIVES, AND ASSESSMENT

We emphasize vocabulary such as *experiment, design, title, variable, independent, dependent, constant, control,* and *conclusion.* As always, teachers can adapt vocabulary activities according to the students' needs and interests.

As an alternative, the students could develop research questions or hypotheses and exchange them with others to design appropriate experiments. Students with a strong

---

Unit Checklist

Name _____

Think about this unit. Choose the best response for every sentence. Did you do a good job? Did the teachers do a good job? What did we learn? Write extra comments at the bottom or on the back.

I understand how I can use the scientific method to solve problems.	Yes	No	Sometimes	Not sure
I understand metric measurement.	Yes	No	Sometimes	Not sure
I understand English measurement.	Yes	No	Sometimes	Not sure
I can observe and describe things well.	Yes	No	Sometimes	Not sure
I can plan an experiment that will answer a question.	Yes	No	Sometimes	Not sure
I worked hard to understand this unit.	Yes	No	Sometimes	Not sure
My teachers worked hard to help me understand this unit.	Yes	No	Sometimes	Not sure
I think other students learned from this unit.	Yes	No	Sometimes	Not sure

I liked:

I didn't like:

How can we do this unit better next year?

science background could research a well-known discovery or experiment, using electronic and print resources, and outline the experiment within the framework of experimental design following a rubric of their own design. They could present their results to the class as a written report, illustrated in a poster, or compiled into a class publication or video on scientific inquiry.

My habit at the end of every grading period has always been to ask students at every level to respond in their journals to variations on the following prompts: "What did we do well this quarter?" "If we could do this all over again, how could we do it better?" Because we encourage students to view teachers as learners and include our performance in their comments, we ask the students to assess not only their own performance but ours as well. Although they could do their assessments in journal form, we use the "Unit Checklist" shown here.

Conclusion

Developing this unit was a challenge, not just because our students come from such varied backgrounds but also because it is the introduction to a year of work that is itself the foundation, conceptually and linguistically, of their science education for the rest of their high school careers. When we developed the unit, we had a rough idea of where the students needed to go, but using standards as a map helped us stay on course and recognize the landmarks along the way.

RESOURCES AND REFERENCES

Classroom Resources

ThinkQuest Junior Team 3804. (1988). *Metrics matter*. Retrieved December 2, 1999, from the World Wide Web: http://tqjunior.advanced.org/3804/index.html.
> *Developed by a student team for the 1998 ThinkQuest Junior Contest, this site contains useful information on English and metric measurement written at an upper elementary level. It also includes a practice activity and simple conversion programs.*

Teacher References

Blair, D. H. (1990). *Science talk: Science in the ESL classroom*. Brattleboro, VT: School for International Training. (ERIC Document Reproduction Service No. ED 326 425)
> *Working with Southeast Asian refugee children, aged 6–12, in the Philippine Refugee Processing Center, the author describes the use of science activities to teach English language. The paper outlines philosophy and theory underlying the approach (particularly the use of the Cognitive Academic Language Learning Approach [CALLA]) as well as describing activities and discussing the approach's relevance to science and language instruction in the United States.*

Chamot, A. U., & O'Malley, J. M. (1994). *The CALLA handbook: Implementing the cognitive academic language learning approach*. Reading, MA: Addison-Wesley.
> *The CALLA model lays out an approach to integrating content and language instruction in order to develop cognitive learning strategies. Chamot and O'Malley offer examples of content instruction. Their section on science shows how it is particularly well suited for language development, allowing for the use of demonstrations and experiments, sequential procedures, and authentic task-based language.*

Commonwealth of Virginia Board of Education. (1995). *Science standards of learning for Virginia public schools*. Retrieved December 2, 1999, from the World Wide Web: http://www.pen.k12.va.us/go/Sols/science.html.
> *This document outlines the goals of the science program through standards of learning for the Commonwealth of Virginia, K–12.*

Fathman, A. K., & Quinn, M. E. (1992). *Teaching science to English learners, Grades 4–8.* Washington, DC: National Clearinghouse for Bilingual Education. (ERIC Document Reproduction Service No. ED 349 844)

Intended for teachers at the middle school level, this document explains the five learning principles proposed by the American Association for the Advancement of Science and clearly ties those principles to principles of language teaching. The document includes steps for designing a science unit as well as three sample activities on heat, animals, and plants.

Gonzales, P. C. (1981). Teaching science to ESL students. *The Science Teacher, 48,* 19–21.

This article addresses several issues for secondary science teachers: the parallels between first and second language acquisition, establishing a learning environment conducive to second language acquisition, and scientific concepts that can serve as foci for instruction of ESOL students.

New Zealand Department of Education. (1986). *Science and second language learners.* Wellington, New Zealand: Author. (ERIC Document Reproduction Service No. ED 334 827)

This document reports the results of a project to develop science materials for use with nonnative speakers of English. It includes suggestions and things to consider when working with English language learners in science classrooms and offers three sample units on the kinesthetic sense, matter, and electricity.

TESOL. (1997). *ESL standards for pre-K–12 students.* Alexandria, VA: Author.

TESOL. (in press). *Scenarios for ESL standards-based assessment.* Alexandria, VA: Author.

UNIT 4
Writing for a Statewide Proficiency Test

PATRICIA HARTMANN

Introduction

It is the beginning of the school year, and the students in the ESL II class have a little more than 8 weeks to prepare for the Ohio Ninth Grade Proficiency Tests. Failure to pass all five parts of the test will result in no high school diploma. So from the first day of school until the end of October, the pressure is on, particularly for Dima, who is a senior and has no desire to spend another year in high school. Dima is almost 18, has been in the United States for almost 2 years, and unfortunately is not a particularly academically inclined student. However, he is very conscious of being a senior and of the need to get all his ducks in a row to graduate.

The proficiency tests are a major obstacle for most ESOL students, at least when they are in the early stages of their English learning. I asked the students in another ESL class, in which most of the students have better English skills and have passed most parts of the test, what they thought about the test. Although one student said, "I'm not so sure about if we need proficiency tests," and another objected "because it is not on specific subject that everyone study," most echoed the sentiments shown in Arthur's writing on the next page.

They thought a lot about which parts of the tests posed the greatest challenges. Violetta wrote, "The most difficult to me is science. To other friends of mine was writing, reading and citizenship. But for me it's science . . . The easies to me was writing. And im not good in writings but I don't know why I liked it the most."

Context

Grade levels: 11th and 12th grades

English proficiency level: Intermediate

Native language of students: Russian

Focus of instruction: English language arts

Type of class: Self-contained, credit-earning ESL class, 50 minutes daily

Length of unit: 4–5 weeks

ARTHUR MEDIS
ESL RESOURCE

> I think the assesment test are use ful
> and are real test. Assesment test show if
> a student learned anything on the lost Junior
> High years and the second one show if a student
> really learned anything in High School. Students
> must show that they learned anything for the
> past years, especially on the subjects that are on
> the test. ESL student should study harder because,
> especially in citizenship because they have no idea
> what it is about. ESL teachers should help ESL
> students on what they need to study for the test.
> Everything is going to be easy if the student studied
> for it. The writing proficiencie is one of the hardest
> especially if your an esl student. you should ask
> help from Mrs. Hartman.

Unit Overview

In Ohio public schools, students must pass all of the Ohio Ninth Grade Proficiency Tests in order to graduate. The five parts are writing, reading, math, citizenship, and science. Students actually take the test for the first time in the spring of the eighth grade. After that, it is administered twice a year, in October and March. The only students who are exempt from the test are those with a special education Individualized Educational Program that specifically excludes such testing. Students who are nonnative speakers of English are allowed extra time to complete the test, and they may use a bilingual dictionary. If a student is in the second semester of the senior year and has attempted but not passed a given part of the test, the district can appeal to the state for an oral administration or for an oral translation of each part of the test except writing.

For most of our ESOL students, the writing section of the test is one of the most difficult. Students must follow the basic conventions of writing if they hope to pass. However, looking beyond the test (and beyond the supposed expectations of ninth-grade writing abilities), the types of writing the test addresses are fundamental formats that students will need for success throughout high school and college.

Particularly in the fall, I organize my ESOL instruction to prepare for the proficiency test. The test may involve three types of writing: narrative, descriptive, and expository. Students will need to respond to prompts such as these, which call for students to write either an essay or a letter:

- One day you wake up to find that you have been magically transformed into a household pet. Tell the story of your adventures that day. Be sure to include specific details of the events you experience after your transformation.

- Many of the holidays we celebrate in the United States are not celebrated elsewhere. The Fourth of July is one of these holidays. In a letter to a friend from another country describe what a typical July 4th celebration is like in your family. Be sure to include details.

- Imagine that you work part-time in a restaurant. One of your coworkers keeps asking you out, but you do not want to go. In a note to your best friend, explain the situation, and explain why you don't want to go out with this person. Lastly, ask your friend for advice about how to handle this problem.

- Write a letter to your English teacher explaining what factors contributed to your low scores on the first writing proficiency test. Discuss your perception of your writing ability, contributing factors on the test, and your strategy for passing the July 15th test. (Ohio Department of Education, 1992, pp. 29–33)

Teachers can easily identify the four prompts as narrative, descriptive, or expository, but of course the student cannot so easily do so. One of the major goals of this unit is to teach the students how to use key words to identify the type of prompt (see the overview below). "Types of Essays" on page 80 (Solon City School District, n.d., n.p.) shows some of these key words.

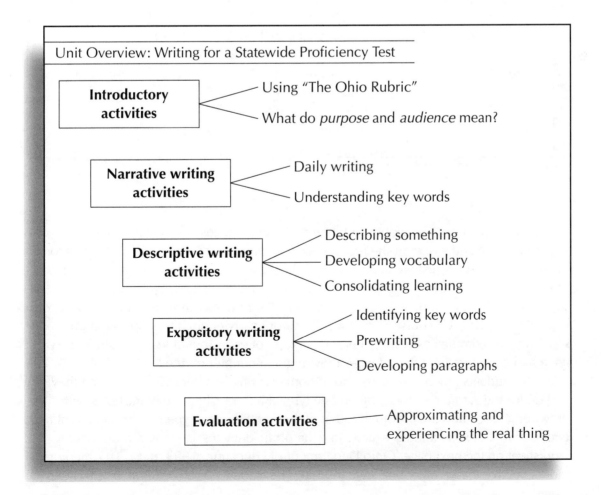

Unit Overview: Writing for a Statewide Proficiency Test

Introductory activities
— Using "The Ohio Rubric"
— What do *purpose* and *audience* mean?

Narrative writing activities
— Daily writing
— Understanding key words

Descriptive writing activities
— Describing something
— Developing vocabulary
— Consolidating learning

Expository writing activities
— Identifying key words
— Prewriting
— Developing paragraphs

Evaluation activities
— Approximating and experiencing the real thing

Types of Essays

All essays Purpose: To communicate to the audience
Be sure to:

- Know what is expected before you begin
- Prewrite/plan
- Answer the question that is asked
- Include details and examples that make your writing come alive

Narrative

Purpose: To tell a story

Key Words:
- experience
- episode
- remember
- relate
- tell
- story
- event

Be sure to:
- Answer the question
- Organize logically (chronologically)
- Include dialogue
- Include specific details

Descriptive

Purpose: To describe a person, place or thing

Key Words:
- describe
- details
- senses
- description

Be sure to:
- Address the question
- Organize spatially
- Include comparisons (similes and metaphors)
- Tell what the object looks like, smells like, tastes like, feels like and sounds like
- Include specific details

Expository

Purpose: To explain something or give information

Key Words:
- explain
- define
- discuss
- prove

Be sure to:
- Use a thesis statement and topic sentences
- Include supporting details that prove your thesis
- Organize your essay by following your thesis statement

During the 4- to 5-week time allotment, the class needs to cover the three types of writing that are addressed on the proficiency test: narrative, descriptive, and expository. I generally spend the first week on narrative, because it is probably the easiest of the three and lends itself well to beginning-of-the-year activities (e.g., "Tell what you did last summer"). After that, I spend about 2 weeks on descriptive writing and then 2 weeks on expository writing. Of course, 1 or 2 weeks is not nearly enough time to spend on something as complex as writing a particular type of essay, but at least the students will have had a taste of the different types they might encounter on the test.

The students practice in-class and at-home writing, shorter than the writing they will do for the actual test, focusing on one type at a time. They use worksheets with prewriting space and the prompt listed at the top of the page, typed in the same font and enclosed in a box, so it looks exactly like the proficiency test (see the sample writing worksheet on the next page; Ohio Department of Education, 1993, p. 8). This medium is more effective than a notebook-style journal. The students become familiar with the

Sample Writing Worksheet

Writing

> Your school newspaper is printing a series of articles about heroes and heroines. Write about someone who is a hero or heroine to you. That person may be someone you know, someone you have read about, a celebrity, or a historical figure. Explain why you believe this person is someone to admire.

STOP.

physical layout and format of the actual test. I include prewriting activities in the unit as well. Setting the writing situation up in this manner encourages the students to prewrite on a regular basis, which they rarely do otherwise.

I also include vocabulary development activities in the unit, as this area is particularly important for any type of description or for prompts requiring the students to "use details." We explore a different vocabulary domain each week, using questions such as "What's another way to say *X*?"

Standards

For 3 years, I have worked to incorporate the standards into my day-to-day teaching and to align them with the other departmental curricula for the district. When I was writing the district curriculum, my first attempts to incorporate standards resulted in quite vague sample progress indicators, such as "Make a checklist," which I assumed that beginning-level students could do.

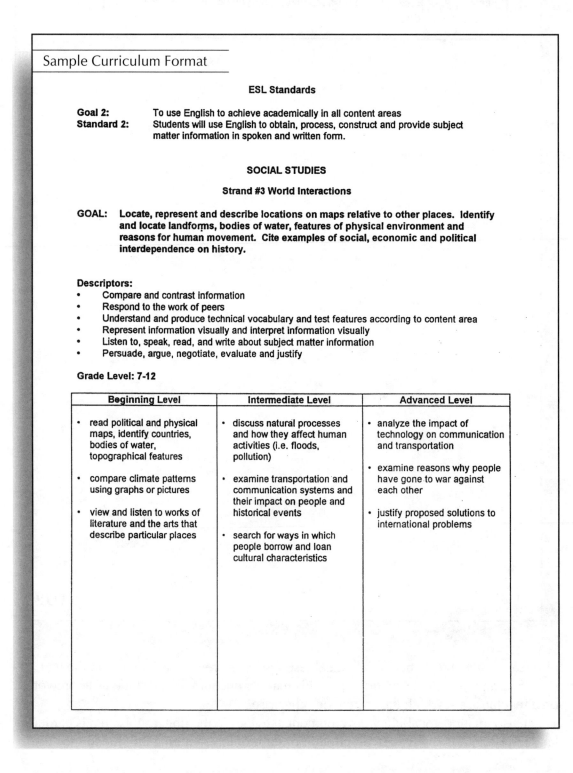

Sample Curriculum Format

ESL Standards

Goal 2: To use English to achieve academically in all content areas
Standard 2: Students will use English to obtain, process, construct and provide subject matter information in spoken and written form.

SOCIAL STUDIES

Strand #3 World Interactions

GOAL: Locate, represent and describe locations on maps relative to other places. Identify and locate landforms, bodies of water, features of physical environment and reasons for human movement. Cite examples of social, economic and political interdependence on history.

Descriptors:
- Compare and contrast information
- Respond to the work of peers
- Understand and produce technical vocabulary and test features according to content area
- Represent information visually and interpret information visually
- Listen to, speak, read, and write about subject matter information
- Persuade, argue, negotiate, evaluate and justify

Grade Level: 7-12

Beginning Level	Intermediate Level	Advanced Level
• read political and physical maps, identify countries, bodies of water, topographical features • compare climate patterns using graphs or pictures • view and listen to works of literature and the arts that describe particular places	• discuss natural processes and how they affect human activities (i.e. floods, pollution) • examine transportation and communication systems and their impact on people and historical events • search for ways in which people borrow and loan cultural characteristics	• analyze the impact of technology on communication and transportation • examine reasons why people have gone to war against each other • justify proposed solutions to international problems

As I worked more with the standards for a state-level ESL instructional guide, I settled on a format for each standard of each goal, as shown in the sample curriculum format from the *South Euclid–Lyndhurst City Schools ESL Course of Study and Handbook* (Brickman, Hartmann, & Watson, 1997, p. 46).

For each standard, we developed brief classroom scenarios, or vignettes, with sample progress indicators for students with limited formal schooling, beginning-level students, intermediate-level students, and advanced-level students. In Ohio, this format works well because a teacher of U.S. history in a mainstream classroom may have a class that includes a small number of ESOL students representing a wide range of English proficiency levels. ESL teaching situations also frequently include students of all levels. It therefore made sense to think about one classroom activity (e.g., building a volcano in a science lab or reading *Romeo and Juliet* in a language arts class) and outline what a beginning-, intermediate-, or advanced-level student could do within the context of that activity. Sample progress indicators for Goal Two, Standard 2 from the *Ohio ESL Instructional Guide* (below; Ohio Lau Resource Center, 1999, p. 3) show how we modified indicators for different student levels.

But even after all that effort, the standards still seemed to be something that lived in a book or, at least, in my head, hovering over my lesson planning, rather than something that was deeply a part of my daily teaching. Then I had a breakthrough: At a Center for Applied Linguistics–sponsored seminar on how to work with teachers to align content standards with the ESL standards, it occurred to me that a good lesson will naturally

Sample Progress Indicators for Goal Two, Standard 2

English Proficiency Level:	No/Little prior Schooling	Beginning	Intermediate	Advanced
Grades 7–8				
Vignette Students are studying about volcanic activity in science class	Arrange pictures of volcanic activity in order of occurrence	Select books from library, identify parts, draw and label picture of active volcano	Explain how a volcano becomes active, with poster or chart	Design a lab experiment, illustrating temperatures and lava flow
Grades 9–12				
Vignette Students are studying World War II	Participate in group making a collage showing different kinds of conflict between people or groups of people	Locate on a map and label countries involved in World War II	In small group, research and list events leading to the war	Interview someone who lived during World War II, and present to class

include at least two of the goals, if not all three, and that the standards will come from there. For example, if the students are talking together in class before the bell rings, that is Goal 1. When they are asking and answering questions in class in the context of the lesson, that is Goal 2. After they leave class and go to the cafeteria and interact with other peers, that is Goal 3.

Although aligning standards may not really be as easy as that, I do feel that much of what we as teachers are already doing is standards-based teaching. However, if we familiarize ourselves more with the standards, we might be able to keep from focusing too intently on tasks that we feel must be done. As a result, we can better concentrate on the student as a whole person.

One final note on taking on the standards in lesson planning: As I work and plan, I keep near me a single page, such as the one shown below (adapted from TESOL, 1997, pp. 9–10), containing all the goals and standards. I find that it makes an easy reference sheet to have handy, rather than having to go through the entire *ESL Standards for Pre-K–12 Students* (TESOL, 1997). Stuck onto this brief list of standards is a note to myself that says, "How does this help me focus on educating the *whole* student as a person?"

ESL Goals and Standards

Goal 1: To use English to communicate in social settings

> ***Standard 1:*** Students will use English to participate in social interactions.

> ***Standard 2:*** Students will interact in, through, and with spoken and written English for personal expression and enjoyment.

> ***Standard 3:*** Students will use learning strategies to extend their communicative competence.

Goal 2: To use English to achieve academically in all content areas

> ***Standard 1:*** Students will use English to interact in the classroom.

> ***Standard 2:*** Students will use English to obtain, process, construct, and provide subject matter information in spoken and written form.

> ***Standard 3:*** Students will use appropriate learning strategies to construct and apply academic knowledge.

Goal 3: To use English in socially and culturally appropriate ways

> ***Standard 1:*** Students will use the appropriate language variety, register, and genre according to audience, purpose and setting.

> ***Standard 2:*** Students will use nonverbal communication appropriate to audience, purpose, and setting.

> ***Standard 3:*** Students will use appropriate learning strategies to extend their sociolinguistic and sociocultural competence.

Introductory Activities

Using the "Ohio Rubric"

The writing proficiency test is scored according to the "Rubric for Scoring Writing" (known as the "Ohio Rubric"; Ohio Department of Education, n.d.). A student can

---

Rubric for Scoring Writing

4   The writing focuses on the topic with ample supporting ideas or examples and has a logical structure. The paper conveys a sense of completeness, or wholeness. The writing demonstrates a mature command of language, including precision in word choice. With rare exceptions, sentences are complete except when fragments are used purposefully. Subject/verb agreement and verb and noun forms are generally correct. With few exceptions, the paper follows the conventions of punctuation, capitalization, and spelling.

3   The writing is generally related to the topic with adequate supporting ideas or examples, although development may be uneven. Logical order is apparent, although some lapses may occur. The paper exhibits some sense of completeness, or wholeness. Word choice is generally adequate and precise. Most sentences are complete. There may be occasional errors in subject/verb agreement and in standard forms of verbs and nouns but not enough to impede communication. The conventions of punctuation, capitalization, and spelling are generally followed.

2   The writing demonstrates an awareness of the topic but may include extraneous or loosely related material. Some supporting ideas or examples are included but are not developed. An organizational pattern has been attempted. The paper may lack a sense of completeness, or wholeness. Vocabulary is adequate but limited, predictable, and occasionally vague. Readability is limited by errors in sentence structure, subject/verb agreement, and verb and noun forms. Knowledge of the conventions of punctuation and capitalization is demonstrated. With few exceptions, commonly used words are spelled correctly.

1   The writing is only slightly related to the topic, offering few supporting ideas or examples. The writing exhibits little or no evidence of an organizational pattern. Development of ideas is erratic, inadequate, or illogical. Limited or inappropriate vocabulary obscures meaning. Gross errors in sentence structure and usage impede communication. Frequent and blatant errors occur in basic punctuation and capitalization, and commonly used words are frequently misspelled.

0   A paper may be considered non-scorable for any of the following reasons:
- Blank Paper
- Illegible/Foreign Language
- Off Topic/Off Task
- Plagiarism
- Refusal
- Insufficient Text
- Erased/Crossed Out

receive a 0 if the writing is illegible or if there is a flagrant disregard of the topic. Students must write two pieces, generally one essay and one letter.

Students need to know how good their writing must be in order to succeed. They need to know what kind of essay constitutes a 4, a 1, or anything in between. The following activity shows students these differences and helps them identify various pregraded essays according to their rating.

Goal 2, Standard 1   To use English to achieve academically in all content areas: Students will use English to interact in the classroom.

Descriptors

- following oral and written directions, implicit and explicit
- participating in full-class, group, and pair discussions
- asking and answering questions
- negotiating and managing interaction to accomplish tasks
- expressing likes, dislikes, and needs

Progress Indicators

- ask a teacher or peer to confirm one's understanding of directions to complete the assignment
- paraphrase a teacher's directions orally or in writing
- share classroom materials and work successfully with a partner
- take turns when speaking in a group

Goal 2, Standard 2   To use English to achieve academically in all content areas: Students will use English to obtain, process, construct, and provide subject matter information in spoken and written form.

Descriptors

- comparing and contrasting information
- evaluating and justifying
- analyzing information
- speaking about subject matter information

Progress Indicators

- locate information appropriate to an assignment in text materials
- organize the appropriate materials needed to complete a task
- take a position and support it in writing
- use contextual clues

PROCEDURE

- Helpful handouts: I give the students a four-page handout that we use throughout the unit. The handout contains "Types of Essays" (p. 80), "Rubric for Scoring Writing" (p. 85), "The Shape of an Essay" (p. 102), and an alternative graphic that shows a more traditional web (p. 103). I simplify the rubric as we go over it, emphasizing that 4 is the best and 1 (or 0) is the worst. The *Resource Manual for Teachers of Writing* (Ohio Department of Education, 1993) gives several sample student essays for each level on the rubric. Each essay was written on the heroes and heroines prompt in the sample writing worksheet shown on page 81.

- Examples: I flip through the manual with the students, showing them briefly what the 4-point essays look like in length and style, then moving through the 3-point, to the 2-point, and on to the 1-point essays. The students are always amused at the poor quality and content of the "1" essays. One of the sample essays discusses people the writer admires: "like Donald Trump man that dude is rollen in money, And Arnold Swarteager he's big and he probably gets all them ladies" (Ohio Department of Education, 1993, p. 49). We touch on the strengths and weaknesses of a few of the other essays.

This part of the activity works much better if the students can work in pairs or small groups, which also allows them to address Goal 2, Standard 2. In addition, it works better if several days have passed since they have first looked at the scores attached to the writing, giving them an opportunity to forget how each essay was originally scored.

- Ratings: I make copies of sample 4-, 3-, 2- and 1-point essays. I give two essays to each of the students and ask them to read the essays silently. I then write *4, 3, 2, 1* across the chalkboard, above which is a cork strip where papers can be posted. After the students read each essay, they go to the board and hang each essay over the score they have chosen. They then have to justify why they gave the essay the grade they did.

When we initially discuss the difference between a score of 0 and a score of 1, we focus on the criterion of illegible handwriting—a particular issue for Dima, whose penmanship is abominable and whose ability to decode cursive writing is also quite limited. When I gave them the essays, the students gave a 0 to all of the ones in cursive because, to the students, the essays were illegible.

- Our own standards: At the end, I give them the actual grades, and we discuss any differences of opinion. We then go back through the *Resource Manual* (Ohio Department of Education, 1993), with the students deciding which sample essays they like, which ones they do not, and why.

Defining *Purpose* and *Audience*

This activity stems from the chart "Types of Essays" (p. 80). The class will be going over three different types of writing that the students will have to do on the proficiency test. Each type of writing has a different purpose, but the words *purpose* and *audience* are initially very vague to the students.

Goal 3, Standard 1   To use English in socially and culturally appropriate ways: Students will use the appropriate language variety, register, and genre according to audience, purpose, and setting.

Descriptors

- using the appropriate degree of formality with different audiences and settings
- recognizing and using standard English and vernacular dialects appropriately
- using a variety of writing styles appropriately for different audiences, purposes, and settings

Progress Indicators

- advise peers on appropriate language use
- express humor through verbal and nonverbal means

PROCEDURE

- Reviewing magazines: I keep a box of old magazines in my room for the students to use when they have collage assignments. Out of this box, I pick one issue of each of the following magazines: *Time, Rolling Stone, Spin, Wired, Newsweek, Sports Illustrated, U.S. News and World Report, Bon Appetit, Country Living, Cooking Light, Smithsonian,* and a publication for tropical fish enthusiasts. We look at the covers and flip through each issue, looking at types of articles and advertisements.

- Finding the purpose: I ask the students to tell me the purpose of each of these magazines. The answers are predictable enough. I hold up *Newsweek,* and Boris says, "To tell news." I hold up the fish magazine, and Dima says, "Talking about fish."

- Thinking about audience: We then discuss the concept of audience. I ask the students, "When you go to a movie, you're watching the screen, and you are the _____." When I ask them how the audiences of *Wired* and *Time* might be different, Boris and Dima agree that the readers of *Wired* are probably younger.

- Defining purpose and audience: We then combine the two concepts of purpose and audience. I write on the board:

  Purpose: What does it do?

  Audience: Who is it for?

  For example, the purpose of *Bon Appetit* is to talk about food, and its

Although this unit begins with narrative writing, moves through descriptive writing, and ends with expository writing, the following activities could be done with any prompt at any point in the unit. A few of the activities lend themselves more to specific types of rhetoric. For example, narratives rely heavily on chronological order. My students do not usually have a very hard time with this concept, so I do not spend much time specifically on chronology activities.

audience is people who enjoy gourmet food. These are different from the purpose and audience of *Rolling Stone* or *Time*.

- We then connect our discussion of these magazines to "Types of Essays":

  the purpose of narrative writing: to tell a story

  the purpose of descriptive writing: to describe something

  the purpose of expository writing: to explain something

Narrative Writing Activities

Narrative writing, as mentioned, is perhaps the easiest type of writing to do. The students all understand the instruction "tell a story about such-and-such."

Daily Writing: Telling Stories as Responses to Prompts

A couple of times a week, the students receive a prompt at the beginning of class. They write in response to the prompt for 15–20 minutes. Afterward, the students share their writing by reading aloud what they have written. I find that this helps students self-correct; if they trip over their words as they are reading, this tips them off that something must be wrong. Discussion follows. Today's prompt has been "Write about a time when you were afraid." Another day it is "Tell about a time when you or someone you know had a disaster with cooking."

When asked, "What does describe mean?" Dima answered, "To tell what it looks like."

> **Goal 2, Standard 2** To use English to achieve academically in all content areas: Students will use English to obtain, process, construct, and provide subject matter information in spoken and written form.

Descriptors

- retelling information
- selecting, connecting, and explaining information
- responding to the work of peers and others
- formulating and asking questions

Progress Indicators

- synthesize, analyze, and evaluate information
- take a position and support it in writing
- edit and revise one's own written assignments
- represent the sequence of events through words
- gather and organize the appropriate materials to complete a task
- consult print resources in the native language when needed

PROCEDURE

- Prompted writing: For the first of these daily writing activities, I select one from a list of prompts designed to elicit narratives and writing about personal experience and write the prompt on the board. Some of the prompts are shown below. Note that they are designed for native-English-speaking students in mainstream language arts classes. Some of these prompts are very challenging to ESOL students, but part of the teaching and learning strategy here is to accustom ESOL students to dealing with these unfamiliar and ambiguous prompts.

> *These activities worked particularly well with a substitute teacher. We all look for activities that a sub can handle, and while I was out for 2 days, she really enjoyed working with them and having the students tell her their stories.*

> Write about a time when you or someone else you know did something very daring.

> Write about a time when you were afraid.

> Write about something that has happened in your school.

> Write about a time when you or someone you know had a disaster with cooking.

> Write about a time when you were not able to face someone or something.

> Write about a time when you were a witness to something important.

> *Although the students could do these essays as homework assignments, I prefer to do them as in-class writings because it more closely simulates the testing situation.*

> Write about the funniest experience you've ever had.

> Re-tell a story you've read or a nursery rhyme you know.

> Write about a frightening or interesting dream you've had. (Ohio Department of Education, 1992, pp. 29–30)

The students spend the next 20 minutes or so writing an essay on the prompt. They may use dictionaries for this practice, just as they may on the test.

- Follow-up: After the students finish writing, they share what they have written. Sometimes the students read their papers aloud; other times they exchange papers and read each other's. At this point in the unit, that is about all they can do. At a later stage, after we have discussed "Types of Essays" and key words, they will know what to watch for as they read and what kinds of things to include as they write. For the prompt, "Write about a time when you or someone you know had a disaster with cooking," two writers produced the memorable stories included here.

Boris Kerzhner 09/15/99

2nd draft - cooking disaster

Sometimes we go hiking.
It was two years ago, in
May. I with my friends, and
my instructor, and went to the
Yral Mountains. It was in
Russia.

We were on the rock clim-
bing competitions? We needed
to eat something before the
competitions started. We also
wanted to drink some tea before the comptitions started also.

Somebody forgot that we were
boiling water for cooking the tea and put some
pasta in the tea.

Another guy put a wet socks
near the tea bag. And this
socks fell down in the tea
bag. So we had a nice tea
with dirty socks and a pasta.

It was funny, but we needed
to drinking this tea, because
we needed to start the
competitions. So how did it
taste

This story about like my father likes to cook.

This story happened in Russian when my mam left haus for kapol day. I was so yang and I dont
remember evrything but I'm go tell you whot I remember. Because this story was so funy.

We sid at home and my and my sister tell my father we wont eat. And my father start cooking .
He was yelt to evryvan because he dasn't no haw to cook. He tuok the very big potato and start clining
after this potato was very smoll. My father he was stay and look on this potato and he sad oryat im not
go no do this im go by sam food like soseg. And you gays go eat this because allredy hav big had aek.

When he tell this story to my mom she was like god I dotn wone hiret this.

Understanding Narrative and Descriptive Key Words

"Types of Essays" (p. 80) helps the students see the connection between the words that are used in the prompt and the type of essay that they have to produce. What confuses the students is that I teach them that they are learning to write a narrative essay and use the term frequently in class, but the word *narrative* occurs nowhere in the prompt. (The students do seem to understand the term *narrator* when the connection is made to a movie or television program in which someone tells the story.) The purpose of this activity, then, is to train the students to recognize the key words within the prompt that tell the purpose of the essay.

The key words are the heart of the unit. The students learn what these words mean and how to differentiate them by color coding each type of writing and the key words that go with it.

Goal 2, Standard 3 **To use English to achieve academically in all content areas: Students will use appropriate learning strategies to construct and apply academic knowledge.**

Descriptors

- focusing attention selectively
- using context to construct meaning
- applying self-monitoring and self-corrective strategies to build and expand a knowledge base
- determining and establishing the conditions that help one become an effective learner (e.g., when, where, how to study)
- evaluating one's own success in a completed learning task

Progress Indicators

- develop an index card system to assist learning
- rehearse and visualize information

PROCEDURE

- Miniquiz: Several days after the students write their narrative pieces, I give them a one-question quiz: "What is the purpose of narrative writing?" All I want in a response is "to tell a story." Dima answers correctly, but when I ask the class to tell me some of the key words under narrative writing, they are unable to do so.

- Pink cards for narrative: I give each student seven pink index cards and tell them to look at the "Types of Essays" chart (p. 80) and copy each of the key words under narrative writing onto a card. We then discuss the meaning of each word. We talk about the different meanings of the word *experience*. The students' immediate association with the term *job experience* is not the right context for narrative writing about an experience. Boris looks up some of the more unfamiliar words in his electronic dictionary, so we are able to use the students' first languages to ensure that the students thoroughly understand the meanings of the words.

- Yellow cards for descriptive: Although the students have not yet studied descriptive writing, producing a set of cards for the corresponding key words at this point solidifies their knowledge about the pink narrative cards and looks ahead to the next essay type. To show the difference between narrative and descriptive writing, I give each student four yellow index cards. On each yellow card, they write the descriptive key words. We discuss them in the same manner.

- Homework: Their homework is to use the narrative and descriptive key words in sentences of their own to show that they understand the meanings. As the homework sample below shows, using new vocabulary in context produces varying results.

Descriptive Writing Activities

Descriptive writing, though seemingly easy to the students, who say, "You just gotta say what something look like," is difficult for that very reason; ESOL students lack the detailed descriptive vocabulary to make their descriptions come alive. Vocabulary development activities therefore enhance this portion of the unit. An excellent source is *Formula Writing 1—Building Toward Writing Proficiency* (Cosner, 1996).

Describing Something in Response to Prompts

Activities to teach description are essentially the same in scope as the first narrative activities in the section Narrative Writing Activities. I explain to the students that they will still be writing an essay but that this time they will be primarily describing, or using lots of details to help a reader picture an object or scene.

PROCEDURE

- Becoming familiar with the prompts: I create a series of prompts that loosely approximate the ones the students might see on the test. Over the next 2 weeks, we work with as many of the prompts as we can. Some I write on the board, and the students write their essays; others we develop as a

---

Homework Sample

1. I did read this story and I think this *story* has a *senses*.
2. I have *experience* to describe a *story*.
3. This *story* has to mach *details*.
4. I go *describe* about school.
5. Did you *remember* how was your first day of school.
6. Tell as a *story* about when you was afraid.
7. *Story* was nice.
8. Did you *event* has *experience* do a *story*.
9. I have *description* for you.

discussion, with the students taking notes, to serve as a model for how to write descriptions. The students do the assignments below as homework. I let them know that a descriptive essay can include elements of narration and that much real-world writing crosses categories.

Tell about your first day of school. [connects narrative with description; the students have to incorporate a little of both]

Describe a chair. [in-class discussion]

Describe something at home, but do not tell me what the thing is.

Describe your best friend, or someone you know very well.

Revise your paper about the disaster with cooking. [incorporates more descriptive language into a narrative piece]

Describe the school cafeteria at lunchtime.

Goal 2, Standard 3   **To use English to achieve academically in all content areas: Students will use appropriate learning strategies to construct and apply academic knowledge.**

Descriptors

- planning how and when to use cognitive strategies and applying them appropriately to a learning task
- actively connecting new information to information previously learned
- imitating the behaviors of native English speakers to complete tasks successfully
- knowing when to use native language resources (human and material) to promote understanding

Progress Indicators

- brainstorm ideas prior to writing a composition on a given topic
- rehearse and visualize information
- seek out print resources in the native language when needed

---

- Evaluation: The last essay serves as a final evaluative writing at the end of the 2 weeks. I see whether the students can incorporate the elements of descriptive writing into a longer, more polished essay. Together, we look for basic elements, such as the presence of more than one paragraph—always a challenge for some students. Writing Sample 1 shows one student's lunchroom essay.

Developing Vocabulary

The idea for vocabulary study based on domains comes from the *Walk, Amble, Stroll* books (Trump, Trechter, & Holisky, 1992, 1995a, 1995b). The goal here is to do textbook work, partly as a break from the intensity of the essay writing the students have been doing. This practice gives them the vocabulary work they need with the added challenge

Writing Sample 1

WRITING SAMPLE 1

Begin Sample 1 Here

My lunch Hour

Evry day has lunch. I love my lunch beca
use i can sio with my prend do my Home work
and take a pood.

In my life i thot two school lunchroom
first in Russia and in U.S. Ite two diprew
lunchRoom. In Russia lunchroom was smool
then in U.S..

In Brush Migth school lunchroom insit
of school. But this room is big rand has a lota
spad. Room has a two room when you can
big a pood. Has a Restroom, Brenkingcound. Tos pure
cool insit smell goot.

In school Nº4 in RussiA diffrent. Because
they has just oune window were you camby
a pood. RestRoom was to far and we don't have
Drinkingpound.

If you need more space, please continue on the back of this page.

3

OHIO DEPARTMENT OF EDUCATION 97-9

(and potential for bonus points) of using their newly acquired vocabulary in their own English writing.

My students and I like working with domains. The grouping of vocabulary by subject allows us to enjoy the richness of the English language—to ponder, for example, the difference between *haze* and *fog* in the unit "How's the Weather" (Trump et al., 1992,

My students are accustomed to vocabulary-in-context work, so learning new words based on words they already know seems natural. They have also heard me say many times, "Use it or lose it!" They know that they need to attempt to use the new vocabulary in their conversations or in writing if they want to remember it.

p. 108). The conversation around degrees of badness (when do we use *appalling, atrocious, wretched, abominable,* or *horrendous?*) allows us to play with language.

Goal 2, Standard 2 **To use English to achieve academically in all content areas: Students will use English to obtain, process, construct, and provide subject matter information in spoken and written form.**

Descriptors

- comparing and contrasting information
- evaluating and justifying
- analyzing information
- speaking about subject matter information

Progress Indicators

- organize vocabulary according to domain
- identify subtle differences between similar vocabulary
- use context to assist in choosing appropriate vocabulary

PROCEDURE

- Exploring the domain: A typical domains unit in the *Walk, Amble, Stroll* series is about 12 pages long and includes a wide variety of opportunities to use the specified language (usually about 20 words). The activities range from simple fill-in-the-blank to many students' favorite activity, in which they decide whether a sentence makes sense or not.

- Writing in response to a prompt: Once we have exhausted the vocabulary, I return to the task at hand and assign a prompt from the list below. I match the prompts with chapters in *Walk, Amble, Stroll.* For example, we do Level 1, chapter 10, "Looking Good and Feeling Good" (Trump et al., 1995a, pp. 98–108), which deals with the domains of looks, weight, and health. After that I assign the prompt "Describe your best friend or a person you know very well."

     Describe your best friend or a person you know very well.

     Describe in full detail the contents and condition of your school locker or a friend's locker.

     Describe a meal that is good for you.

     Describe your favorite athlete.

     Describe your favorite private space.

     Describe coming to life in spring.

     Describe an ordinary object to someone who has never seen it.

     Describe a homeless, hungry dog or cat.

     Describe someone who is famous.

Describe your own neighborhood.

Describe a parade on the Fourth of July. (Ohio Department of Education, 1992, pp. 30–31)

- Rewarding vocabulary use: Because the students' work on a given domain has sensitized them to language, it is easy for them to incorporate new vocabulary. Sometimes I ask the writer or a classmate reader to highlight the domain vocabulary that is in a piece of student writing. I award extra points to both the writer and the reader for every domain word thus highlighted.

Consolidating the Students' Learning and Looking Ahead

Before Open House in the fall, I need to create displays on my bulletin boards. I ask the students to make a poster or bulletin board display of "Types of Essays." This activity gives them the opportunity to review the two types of writing that they have already studied and, with my help, to look ahead to the third type.

The students' use of English during this activity leads me to call it a Goal 1 activity. One fall, Boris and Dima were sitting at the computer, deciding how they would type up this information for the bulletin board (what size, what font, and so forth). Much of the conversation was in their native language, Russian, but it was interspersed with terminology in English. I found this fine example of code switching highly entertaining, but it also seemed to help the students understand better.

Goal 1, Standard 3 To use English to communicate in social settings: Students will use learning strategies to extend their communicative competence.

Descriptors

- listening to and imitating how others use English
- exploring alternative ways of saying things
- using the primary language to ask for clarification
- learning and using language "chunks"
- practicing new language

Progress Indicators

- ask a classmate whether a particular word or phrase is correct
- use a computer spell checker to verify spelling
- test appropriate use of new vocabulary, phrases, and structures
- ask someone the meaning of a word

PROCEDURE

- Typing the terms: The students work in pairs at a computer, using a word-processing or presentation program to enter the names of the different types of essays, their purposes, and the key words, and using different fonts, type sizes, and type styles for each. Pairing the students automatically generates conversation that focuses on what to do, how to use the computer, how to design the words, and how to correct errors.

- Preparing a display: The students cut out the individual words and glue them to appropriately colored paper (pink for narrative, yellow for descriptive, and blue for expository). Finally, they organize their work into an attractive display and put it up.

Expository Writing Activities

Identifying Key Words in Prompts

Now that the students are familiar with the key words, the next step is applying this knowledge: finding and recognizing the key words within a prompt, and then identifying what type of writing (narrative, descriptive, or expository) is required.

PROCEDURE

- Determining the essay type: I give the students copies of several practice prompts. They then discuss among themselves which prompts require narrative writing, which descriptive, and which expository.

- Confirming their choice: To substantiate their decisions, they find the key words in the prompts, going back to "Types of Essays" or their colored cards.

At this point, the students often ask if they can take the colored index cards with them to the actual test. Although they cannot bring in extra materials, I tell them to visualize and remember what colors have what words on them.

> **Goal 2, Standard 2** To use English to achieve academically in all content areas: Students will use English to obtain, process, construct, and provide subject matter information in spoken and written form.
>
> ### Descriptors
> - negotiating, evaluating, and justifying
> - analyzing, synthesizing, and inferring from information
> - speaking and reading about subject matter information
> - demonstrating knowledge through application
> - understanding technical vocabulary and text features
>
> ### Progress Indicators
> - locate information appropriate to an assignment in text materials
> - synthesize, analyze, and evaluate information
> - take a position and support it in writing
> - use contextual clues
> - utilize a chart synthesizing information

Goal 2, Standard 3 To use English to achieve academically in all content areas: Students will use appropriate learning strategies to construct and apply academic knowledge.

Descriptors

- focusing attention selectively
- applying basic reading comprehension skills such as skimming, scanning, previewing, and reviewing text
- using context to construct meaning
- determining and establishing the conditions that help one become an effective learner (e.g., when, where, how to study)

Progress Indicators

- evaluate a written assignment using rating criteria provided by the teacher
- skim to determine key points of a text
- scan an entry to locate information for an assignment

Prewriting

Most of my ESOL students skip the prewriting step. I think they view it as unnecessary, even as a waste of time. Teachers, of course, realize the importance of prewriting to generate ideas and organize thoughts. Students need to be taught specifically how to gather their ideas and words.

PROCEDURE

- Teaching strategies: *Academic Writing: Techniques and Tasks* (Leki, 1989) and *Roots in the Sawdust* (Gere, 1985) have excellent information on different types of prewriting, such as **cubing,** listing, **webbing**, free writing, and brainstorming. I demonstrate each one of these methods on the board as a model for the students.

- Applying strategies: I give one prompt from the list below to the class and assign each student a different method of prewriting on that idea. For example, if the prompt asks the writer to describe winter, one student may do a web, one student may use cubing, and another student might make a list. They then compare their ideas.

  Tell how to be a perfect brother or sister.

  Tell how to be a perfect parent.

  Explain how to become a computer expert.

  Tell how to become a winning athlete.

  Think of a problem you have had and tell how you solved it.

  Write about the different kinds of music and musicians.

Tell why brothers and sisters sometimes fight with one another.

Tell what effects TV and movie violence have on kids.

Compare life in school to life during summer vacation. (selected from Ohio Department of Education, 1992, pp. 31–33)

Goal 2, Standard 3 To use English to achieve academically in all content areas: Students will use appropriate learning strategies to construct and apply academic knowledge.

Descriptors

- focusing attention selectively
- applying basic reading comprehension skills such as skimming, scanning, previewing, and reviewing text
- planning how and when to use cognitive strategies and applying them appropriately to a learning task

Progress Indicators

- visualize information
- scan an entry in a book to prepare for an assignment
- apply specific strategies to prepare for a task
- examine and evaluate different methods to accomplish the same task
- explain and expand oral information to check comprehension

Developing Paragraphs of the Expository Essay Using Graphic Organizers

At this point in the unit, the formatting and the organization of the essay become most important. When I teach the expository essay, I focus on "The Shape of an Essay" (Solon City School District, n.d., n.p.), shown on page 102, and the fact that an essay needs to have an introduction, five paragraphs (each about a different facet of the main idea), and a conclusion. This is the most difficult part of the unit. I use a lot of visuals to reinforce the arrangement of the pieces of this essay.

As we develop our expository essay, we work simultaneously with two topics—Grandma as hero (the model essay) and the reasons they came to the United States (the students' own essays). Addressing two topics at the same time seems to highlight the essential elements of the essay, the parts that must be present in both.

Procedure

- Reviewing a model essay: We start with a homework assignment, a sample essay found in the *Resource Manual* (Ohio Department of Education, 1993, pp. 11–13) that

The students often say—incorrectly—that the model expository essay is descriptive. They defend their choice by pointing to all the details.

addresses the prompt to write about a hero or heroine. The students reread the essay and decide whether it is narrative, descriptive, or expository writing. My task is to show them that this type of essay generally can be identified by the presence of a thesis statement and that the next paragraphs are connected to that thesis statement.

Goal 2, Standard 3   To use English to achieve academically in all content areas: Students will use appropriate learning strategies to construct and apply academic knowledge.

Descriptors

- focusing attention selectively
- applying basic reading comprehension skills such as skimming, scanning, previewing, and reviewing text
- using context to construct meaning
- determining and establishing the conditions that help one become an effective learner (e.g., when, where, how to study)

Progress Indicators

- evaluate a written assignment using rating criteria provided by the teacher
- skim to determine key points of a text
- scan an entry to locate information for an assignment
- expand on written information to check comprehension
- verbalize relationships between new and previously learned information

---

- Taking the essay apart: I copy the template from "The Shape of an Essay" onto the board and write the same essay's thesis statement in the top triangle. I write the thesis statement in blue chalk on the board to reinforce that this is an expository essay. I also reinforce that these triangular and rectangular shapes are the building blocks of an essay. The students' homework is to tell me the three main ideas that the writer says about Grandma.

- Adding details: The next day, I again copy the shapes on the board. We add the main ideas in the rectangles and discuss the details of each paragraph. For some students, a web such as the one shown on page 103, which indicates places for details, is an additional help.

- Preparing to write: For homework, the students prepare to write an expository essay of their own. I ask them to think of three reasons their family came to the United States.

- Analyzing their own writing: The next day, on the board, we fill in the three main reasons (one for each rectangle) the students' families came to the

The Shape of an Essay

The Shape of an Essay

introdaction

fat wanted to make a lot of money
in school, programmer, math.

I wouldn't have to join the Army
you have to serve for two years
age 18.

Young people can work here.
No part time jobs for students in Russia

Conclusion.

United States. The students fill in their own information on their own copy of "The Shape of an Essay."

- Writing their own essay: For homework, the students put the main ideas and details about why their families came to the United States into an essay. Two sample essays are included on pages 104–105.

Students often complain that introductions and conclusions are hard to write. After a little prodding, they generally agree that it is better to have something than to have nothing. We discuss the triangle representation of general to specific, noting the general first sentence of the model hero essay, saying that young people need heroes, moving to the thesis statement, which is that Grandma has been a big influence and is someone to admire.

Evaluation Activities

Approximating and Experiencing the Real Thing

At the end of the activities on each type of writing, I give an in-class practice proficiency test. The first experience, at the end of the narrative segment, involves some discussion and a little less writing. By the second segment, I attempt to more closely simulate the

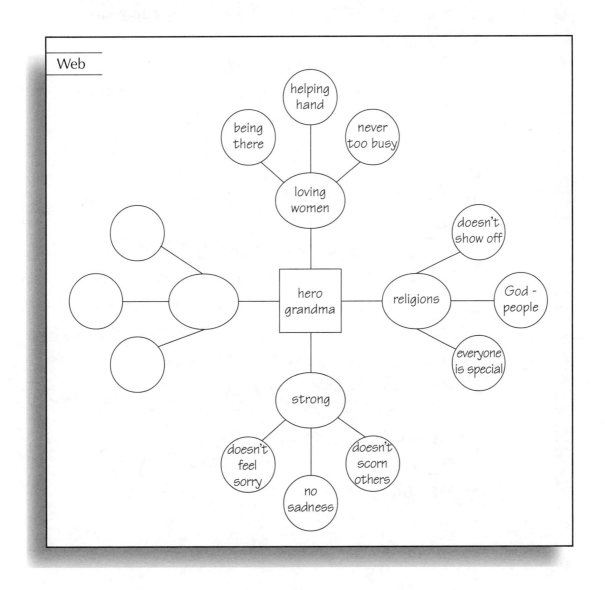

Boris Kerchner.
09/29/99.

There are a lot of people who came in America from another countries. There are many russian people, Chinese people, Japanese people and other people. Our family came to America, because the life in America better, than in ~~Russia~~ Russia ~~other~~

Our family came to America, because my father could make a lot of money here. He is a programmer. He could made 50.000 dollars in a year. For example in Russia he made 625 dollars in year.

There are no army for you in America if you don't want it. Everybody has two years army in Russia and 0.5 of those people don't come back see their parents after army.

Young people can work in America after 14 years old. They can do not really big money, but they can bought a

continued on p. 105

Sample Essays, *continued*

car and another things. You can work in Russia after 18 years old. But it's very difficut to get any job in Russia. It's big problem for young people. I prefer live in America than in Russia, but I'm sure, that some times I will be have a vacations in Russia. I want to spend time with my friends some times.

My resin to came in U.S. was very big. Ferstabl my mam's family live here My mather miss they and call to as and they tell as cam to U.S.. My casein olives call my and tell my cam here because here is mach beater.

Second resin why I came here was a life in Russia is hard. My percents has no job because hall factories and stores close. People work there and didn't get pay for this job. People can not faund job because evrythynk close.

When I finish high school I think about collage. But that diploma I don't need my because I can not get good pay. Teachers wasn't tech as because they not get pay for. In a winter can be cold because govertmen didn't won to pay for.

actual proficiency test: The students write on worksheets that look like the proficiency test, under test conditions, with no talking allowed. With the third and final essay the students have come full circle: They once again encounter the hero prompt they saw at the beginning of the unit. Now, however, they have to write their own essay on that topic.

PROCEDURE

- The last practice test: I give the students the hero expository prompt (see p. 81) and the special proficiency test writing paper. They have the entire class period to write their essays. I try to schedule this final activity for the Friday before the actual test. Dima already knows that he has come a long

Ohio Department of Education. (1995). *Practice test for the Ohio Ninth-Grade Proficiency Tests.* Columbus, OH: Author.

> *This publication is designed for students preparing for the tests as well as for their teachers. The sample tests are about half the length of the actual tests.*

Ohio Department of Education. (n.d.). *Instructions for administering the Practice Test for the Ohio Ninth-Grade Proficiency Tests* (p. 10). Columbus, OH: Author. Retrieved June 10, 2000, from the World Wide Web: http://www.ode.ohio.gov/www/ae9instruc.pdf.

Sebranek, P., Meyer, V., & Kemper, D. (1996). *Writers INC: A student handbook for writing and learning.* Wilmington, MA: Great Source Education Group.

> *This excellent resource book is used in the Solon City School District's Grade 9–12 mainstream language arts curriculum.*

Smalley, R. L., & Ruetten, M. K. (1990). *Refining composition skills: Rhetoric and grammar for ESL students* (3rd ed.). Boston: Heinle & Heinle.

> *This college-level ESL writing text breaks down its chapters by rhetorical modes. Instruction is given on both paragraph and essay development.*

Tong, D. (1997). *Pass in a flash: Reading/writing flash cards, Grade 9.* Columbus, OH: Englefield & Arnold.

> *These flash cards, designed for the Ohio Ninth Grade Proficiency Tests in reading and writing, offer a different type of visual and tactile medium for students to study.*

Trump, K., Trechter, S., & Holisky, D. A. (1992). *Walk, amble, stroll: Vocabulary building through domains, Level 2.* Boston: Heinle & Heinle.

> *This vocabulary development text is intended for intermediate-level learners.*

Trump, K., Trechter, S., & Holisky, D. A. (1995a). *Walk, amble, stroll: Instructor's manual, Level 1 and Level 2.* Boston: Heinle & Heinle.

> *This manual consists of reproducible unit reviews and answer keys for all chapters in both levels.*

Trump, K., Trechter, S., & Holisky, D. A. (1995b). *Walk, amble, stroll: Vocabulary building through domains, Level 1.* Boston: Heinle & Heinle.

> *This vocabulary development text is intended for high beginning-level students.*

Teacher References

Brickman, R., Hartmann, P., & Watson, J. (1997). *South Euclid–Lyndhurst City Schools ESL course of study and handbook.* Lyndhurst, OH: South Euclid–Lyndhurst City School District. (Available from South Euclid–Lyndhurst City School District, 5044 Mayfield Road, Lyndhurst, OH 44124; http://www.state.oh.us/proficiency)

Gere, A. I. (Ed.). (1985). *Roots in the sawdust: Writing to learn across the disciplines.* Urbana, IL: National Council of Teachers of English.

> *This text and accompanying materials were used at my high school for a professional development course on writing across the curriculum.*

Ohio Department of Education. (1992). *Intervention module for the Ninth Grade Proficiency Test, Language Arts: Reading and Writing.* Columbus, OH: Author.

> *This packet offers mainstream language arts teachers suggestions on preparing students for the test. It lists many practice prompts for each type of writing required on the test.*

Ohio Lau Resource Center. (1999). Update on the *Ohio ESL Instructional Guide. Ohio Lau Resource Center Update, 3*(1), 3.

> *When published, the* Ohio ESL Instructional Guide *will provide standards-based accommodations for ESL and content teachers of beginning-, intermediate-, and advanced-level ESL students.*

Solon City School District. (n.d.). *Writing proficiency.* Unpublished packet.

> *This packet provides many of the charts and graphic organizers that I use in my class.*

TESOL. (1997). *ESL standards for pre-K–12 students.* Alexandria, VA: Author.

UNIT 5
Autobiographical Writing

SANDRA BRIGGS

Introduction

On a selected day, every student in Grades 9–11 in the San Mateo Union High School District (SMUHSD) is writing an essay known as the District Essay Competency Exam. In the ESL 4 class in Room 74 at Burlingame High School on that day, 24 are students writing quietly. Some are looking up words in English or bilingual dictionaries; some are writing quick notes to themselves before they start in on their essays; others have already started their draft writing; one or two have hands raised because they want to talk to me. But all of them are confident and prepared for this day. Although they are not in a mainstream English class, and although some of them have only been in the United States for a few months, they have learned how to make the most out of the English they do have. Each one of them will write something interesting and relevant to the topic.

When they give their exams to me, I will read them quickly and then put them in an envelope to send to the district office. Some time in the next 6 weeks, a group of teachers and administrators from the district will read the exams and evaluate them. On a scale of 0–6, 3 is the magic number. It means that the student has passed at a minimal level and has fulfilled that graduation requirement. After all of our preparation, we want

---

Context

Grade levels: 9th–12th grades

English proficiency level: High intermediate

Native languages of students: Spanish, Mandarin, Cantonese, Japanese, Tagalog, Korean, Farsi

Focus of instruction: ESL/writing

Type of class: ESL, double class period

Length of unit: 3 weeks

to know right now who has passed, but we will have to wait a long time. I tell my students not to worry; they have done their best, and that is what counts. I am proud of all of them for learning how to write to a prompt, showing what they can do in English. If they do not pass this time, there is always next year.

Unit Overview

Just as social studies, math, and science are content areas for ESOL students, so are mainstream English literature and writing. The mainstream English teachers and the ESL teachers can cooperate and play important roles in assisting ESOL students as they cross the bridge from advanced ESL to mainstream English. We know that ESOL students need to enter mainstream English classes with a great deal of experience in how to read and analyze literature, but what about writing? Do not all students write in all of their classes and all teachers work with students on writing? And have ESOL students not been writing in English since their days as beginners? Of course they have, but ESOL students also need to be prepared for the specific types of writing that students do in all of their classes and, in the situation I describe here, for the writing they need to do on demand as a graduation requirement. However, the emphasis in this unit is much more on autobiographical writing than on preparing for the exam.

In the SMUHSD, all students are required to pass a writing competency exam before they graduate. All 9th- through 11th-grade students take the appropriate level of this exam each year, even if they wrote at a passing level in an earlier year. Twelfth-grade students who have not yet passed the exam also take it. All students in ESL classes take the 9th-grade exam, and in the ESL 4 class, teachers prepare the students for this experience. It is a part of the writing strand at this level.

The autobiographical writing unit goals dovetail with the semester writing goals: Students will demonstrate the ability to

- use process writing, which includes brainstorming, organizing, drafting, editing, proofreading, and producing a final draft
- control word choice, sentence structure, verb forms, spelling, and punctuation well enough so that their writing can be understood by native speakers of English
- write a formal essay that includes an introduction, development through details/examples, and a conclusion

The unit goals are as follows: Students will demonstrate the ability to

- use a writing prompt to guide the development of a piece of writing
- participate in class and group discussions to clarify and organize ideas on writing about autobiographical incidents
- produce a draft of an autobiographical incident that shows emotions and character through dialogue and action
- edit and proofread individually and in groups
- produce a good first draft of an autobiographical incident in a timed situation

I developed this unit on autobiographical writing not so much to prepare the students for the District Essay Competency Exam as to take advantage of a real-world situation to help the students build confidence in how they can use what they already know about English, about themselves, and about biographies and autobiographies to produce a piece of writing that they can be proud of. ESOL students who are about to enter mainstream English classes at Burlingame High School have to demonstrate the ability to look at a writing assignment and figure out what the purpose is, who the audience is, and what kind of writing they need to do to successfully complete the assignment. They have received lots of support in their ESL classes; now they need to understand how they can take what they have done in ESL and do it on their own.

The unit overview shows the sequence of activities for the 3-week unit.

Standards

Planning lessons is not a linear task for me. I view my planning as in the Venn diagram on the next page (from TESOL, in press). Once I have a starting point, I think in all directions and begin to build a unit and lessons. A unit may start from an idea for an activity that I get from a colleague, a conference presentation, an article, or my students. After I try it out in class, if it has potential, I may develop it into a unit. Or I may start

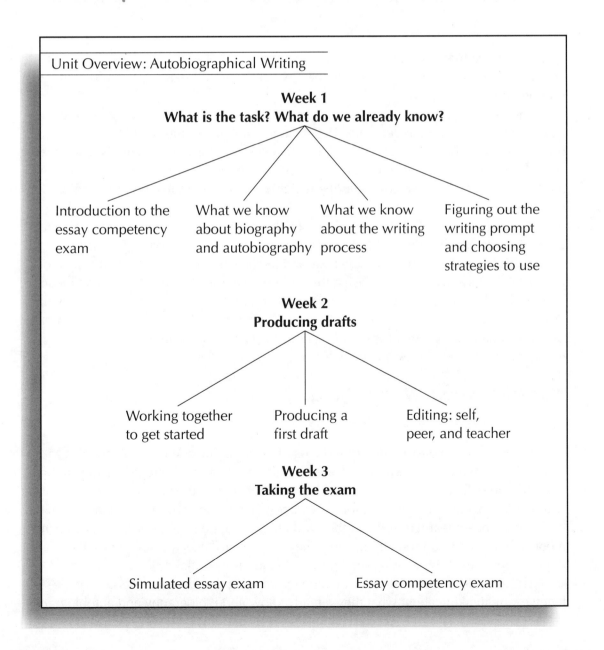

Unit Overview: Autobiographical Writing

Week 1
What is the task? What do we already know?

Introduction to the essay competency exam

What we know about biography and autobiography

What we know about the writing process

Figuring out the writing prompt and choosing strategies to use

Week 2
Producing drafts

Working together to get started

Producing a first draft

Editing: self, peer, and teacher

Week 3
Taking the exam

Simulated essay exam

Essay competency exam

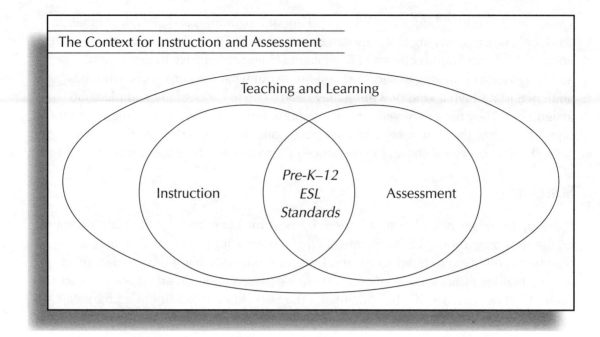

The Context for Instruction and Assessment

Teaching and Learning

Instruction

Pre-K–12 ESL Standards

Assessment

from a standard that my students need to meet, figuring out what activities I can use to help the students get there. In this unit, the District Essay Competency Exam was the starting point.

The planning process I went through might be mapped out something like the lesson-planning chart included here. The standards link me to the world beyond my own classroom. They help me work with colleagues, administrators, parents, and other education professionals. They help me answer the questions, Where are we going? Will this activity lead where we are going? How does what I want to teach fit into the big picture?

When the SMUHSD ESL Council revised the district master plan, the raw materials were *ESL Standards for Pre-K–12 Students* (TESOL, 1997) and standards from other sources, the former program, and the texts and lessons that teachers at different schools in the district have used. After revising the program, we developed rubrics so that teachers can decide when students have met the exit criteria for each of the four levels in the program. At this writing, the rubric is still in draft form, but I use it as one of the evaluation tools in this autobiographical writing unit. My experience will help the council refine the rubric and also improve my lessons.

Activities, Week 1: What Is the Task? What Do We Already Know?

The students need to clearly understand what they are being asked to do and why. In fact, I always start out a new unit or lesson by discussing why we are doing something, how it fits into the overall plans for the class, and what the students already know that will help them with the unit or lesson. They know that we are working together to make them independent learners and that they will always get the instructions, materials, and models they need to do something well. They have heard me say many times that thinking about the best learning strategies for the job is essential.

The activities in this first week include introducing the idea of the essay competency exam; thinking about what they already know about biography and autobiography

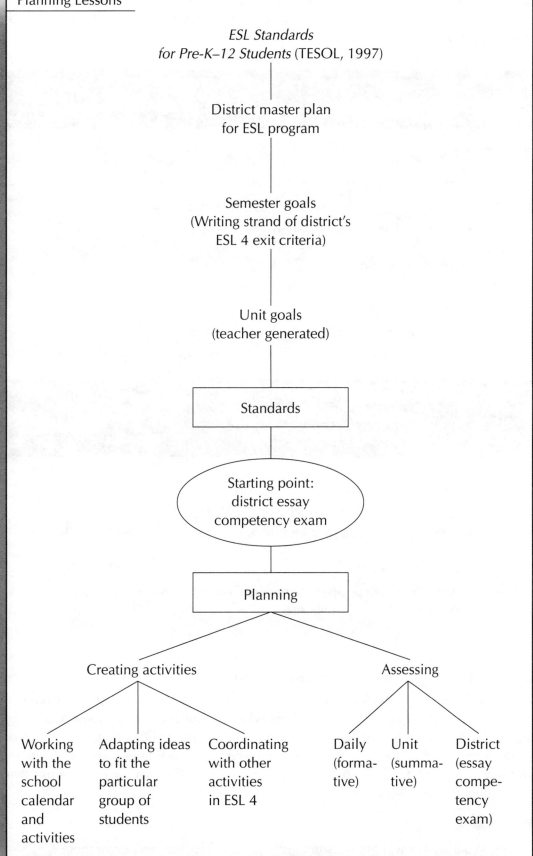

ESL Standards
for Pre-K–12 Students (TESOL, 1997)

District master plan
for ESL program

Semester goals
(Writing strand of district's
ESL 4 exit criteria)

Unit goals
(teacher generated)

Standards

Starting point:
district essay
competency exam

Planning

Creating activities   Assessing

Working   Adapting ideas   Coordinating   Daily   Unit   District
with the   to fit the   with other   (forma-   (summa-   (essay
school   particular   activities   tive)   tive)   compe-
calendar   group of   in ESL 4   tency
and   students   exam)
activities

and working with one or two examples that help them focus on how they can write about themselves; reviewing what they know about the writing process; figuring out what to do with the kind of writing prompt they will be given; and, finally, choosing the strategies they will need to do this kind of writing.

Goal 2, Standard 1 To use English to achieve academically in all content areas: Students will use English to interact in the classroom.

Descriptors

- requesting and providing clarification
- participating in full-class, group, and pair discussions
- asking and answering questions

Progress Indicators

- ask a teacher or peer to confirm one's understanding of directions to complete an assignment
- ask a teacher to restate or simplify directions

Goal 2, Standard 3 To use English to achieve academically in all content areas: Students will use appropriate learning strategies to construct and apply academic knowledge.

Descriptors

- focusing attention selectively
- actively connecting new information to information previously learned

Progress Indicator

- verbalize relationships between new information and information previously learned in another setting

---

Introduction to the Essay Competency Exam

I find that it helps students focus on the work when they take notes based on what I write on the board while I am talking about what the students will be doing and why. It also gives them a written record to refer to when they are working. I often ask the students to write in their journals after we have discussed something important that they will have to do or after they have completed a project or task. This activity helps them clarify how they feel about the task.

PROCEDURE

- What we know: I ask the students to go to the writing section of their binders and take out paper for note-taking. I write "District Essay Competency Exam" on the board and ask what they know about this exam.

As the students offer ideas or raise questions, we talk about them, and I write some of them on the board for the students to copy.

- What the exam is like: When the students have given all their suggestions, we look at what I have written, and I tell them what the exam will be like, when it will be given, and what we will do to prepare for it. I emphasize that they already know how to go about this task and that we will do a short review of autobiographical writing and the writing process as they get ready to practice for the exam.

- How they feel: We pass out the students' journals, and they write about how they feel about this exam. Are they scared or excited? What kinds of questions do they have about it? What have they heard about it from their friends? The students write for about 15 minutes and then put their journals back in the journal box. We talk a little bit about their questions and ideas, and that evening I read their journals and respond to their enthusiasm to work on the task, their willingness to prepare for it, and their concerns. I address some of the concerns that come up in many of the journals the next day in class. I never quote directly from anyone's journal or talk about what individual students write without asking their permission first.

What We Know About Biography and Autobiography

The students have had varying experiences with biography and autobiography before I start this unit. We have read some examples in class, and some students have read biographies and autobiographies as part of their free-choice reading. We discuss what they know about this subject, read a selection together, and brainstorm what they will want to include if they write about themselves or about other people.

Many biographies and autobiographies are written at a level that is accessible to intermediate- to advanced-level ESOL students. Good fiction told in the first person and based on the author's experiences certainly qualifies as autobiography for the purposes of this unit. *The House on Mango Street* (Cisneros, 1984) and Soto's (1985) writings about growing up in Fresno, California, are always class favorites. We talk about how authors draw on their own experiences to create characters. It is a good way to show that the students do not always have to tell the exact truth about what happened when they write. Our class library has many of these books (see Resources and References at the end of this unit). In this activity I use *The Language of Literature: Blue Level* (Boley, Golub, & McBride, 1997) to look at the differences between biography and autobiography and different styles. The students' favorite selection is the one about Malcolm X. I emphasize **show, don't tell** in our students' writing, so I look for passages that are full of details as the best examples.

Procedure

- Defining terms: I write *biography* on the board and ask the students to tell me about it. We discuss the term, and they give me examples that they have read or heard about. When I write *autobiography* on the board, they can tell me that it means writing about oneself. They give examples. I ask them to think about what writers do when they write biography. They have a few ideas, but they are a little unclear on the concept, so I suggest that we read a piece of biographical or autobiographical writing and think about what the author did.

- Preparing to work: I want the students to read a short piece with another student, focusing on what the author does in biography. I often use a **clock of partners** to divide the students into pairs quickly. Once a semester, the students write their names in spaces corresponding to the hours on each other's paper clocks. They can write another student's name only once or twice on the clock, so they work with a variety of partners. I ask the students to take out their clocks, but I do not tell them which partner they are going to work with until they all understand the instructions. (As soon as I announce which partner they are working with, they are focused on working with that person rather than on the instructions.)

- Reading a selection: As we talk about the instructions, I make a short list on the board:

  > Go to your partner with the book, paper, and a pen or a pencil.

  > Take turns reading the selection by paragraphs, stopping after each paragraph to discuss it.

  > On one piece of paper with both names on it, make a list of how Malcolm X told the story of learning to read in prison.

  > Write down any questions you have about the selection.

  > Finish in about 20 minutes.

- Pairing up: After we discuss the directions and pass out the books, I ask the students to go to their 3 o'clock partner. If they do not have a 3 o'clock partner or if their partner is absent, they come to the front of the room to be paired up. Once everyone is working, I circulate around the room listening and watching, but I do not interfere with the pairs unless they raise their hands to ask for me or I see that a pair is having a lot of trouble.

- Sharing results: When most students have had enough time to finish, we talk about what they have learned. The class list includes such items as

  > Malcolm told why he wanted to learn to read.

  > He used his friend's words.

  > He told about the problem.

  > He told what he did about the problem.

  > He showed how he felt: He was excited and frustrated.

  > He gave details with names.

  The students copy the class's list to help them with their writing.

- Assessing the students' work: I collect the students' lists, give the students points for their work, comment on their ideas, and return the lists the next day. We talk about what we have learned from this work.

> In all classes, we as teachers should be sensitive to what we ask students to tell us about their lives. Many students have nontraditional families and have had difficult experiences that they are naturally reticent to share. Any time I ask students to draw on their own lives, I point out that they do not have to tell everything and that they can invent and change the situation somewhat. I also allow them to be like authors Sandra Cisneros and Gary Soto; they can use their life experience to invent characters and situations.

What We Know About the Writing Process

By the time that we start this unit, the students have already done a number of pieces of process writing. They have folders in the room, with their names on them, in which they keep copies of writing they have done. Most of the time, they have stapled the brainstorming sheets, drafts, and editing comments to their final draft.

PROCEDURE

- Reviewing process writing: I ask the students to tell me the steps in the writing process. They all know them. As they tell me, I write the steps on the board. We discuss what is involved in each step:

  1. brainstorming
  2. organizing
  3. drafting
  4. editing
  5. rewriting
  6. proofreading
  7. preparing the final draft

- Customizing process writing to the task: The students and I have talked before about variations in the writing process. Because we always think about learning strategies and different styles of working and learning, we have already talked about times when writers will modify the process. This time, I ask the students how they think the process will be different in writing this essay exam. They volunteer that they will not have time to do much brainstorming and that they cannot make a draft and then a final copy. They also know that they can use dictionaries but cannot ask classmates or teachers for help. They are worried that they will not be able to do this. I tell them that many ESL 4 students have done it before and that they will practice so that they will be ready.

Figuring Out the Writing Prompt and Choosing Strategies to Use

The students do not know ahead of time what the topic on the exam will be, and they do not practice with the actual exam questions. However, I prepare sample prompts so that the students will know how to read the instructions and what to do with them. One sample writing prompt is included on the next page.

PROCEDURE

- Examining the prompt: I ask the students to take out their clock of partners. I explain that we are going to look at a practice prompt for the essay exam and that I want them to figure out what the prompt asks them to do and how they will go about doing it. I pass out the prompt and give them a few minutes to read it to themselves. Then I ask them to go to their partners and discuss the prompt for 4 minutes. I tell them which partner to go to, and they get to work.

- Sharing interpretations: When the class comes back together, I ask for volunteers to tell the class what the prompt asks them to do and how they would go about it. There are many different answers and some disagreements about what they are supposed to do. Some students think that

Sample Writing Prompt

Writing Prompt
ESL 3-4: Writing
Autobiography: Coming to America

Writing Situation

One of the major changes you have experienced was the move to California in the United States. You may have felt happy or sad when the decision was made to move. You may have had a funny or scary trip here. You may have had some problems with the culture or language when you first arrived.

Directions for Writing

Write about an incident that occurred when you came to the United States. You may choose to write about either the decision to come, the trip over, or a problem you had in settling into the new place. Include many details about the people, places, and events that happened. Be specific, use sensory images, and include dialogue. Help the reader re-live your story with you.

they need to write one essay for the writing situation and another for the directions for writing. Some think that they have to tell the whole story of their trip here. Some of them say that their trip was not exciting enough; they just got on an airplane and came here. When I ask them what an incident is, they are not sure.

- Planning the writing: I ask them to take out paper on which to take notes on the prompt. I tell them that the writing situation is background information. It is there to help them think about the situation and decide on an incident that they can write about. We look for the code words in the actual directions. I explain that an incident usually takes place within 24 hours. The students can refer to events that occurred before or after that time, but the writing needs to have a frame. It needs to focus on one important event. I give them an example of something that does not have a focus or a time frame: "Someone is thinking about coming to the United States and then he didn't come for a long time and then his parents asked him if he wanted to come and he thought about it for a few months and then . . . ." The students get the idea that in describing an incident the writer does not want to string together events without focus.

- Thinking about details: The directions also ask for details, specificity, sensory images, and dialogue. We talk about each of these and give examples that the students copy into their notes so that they can use them when they write.

- Thinking about strategies: We talk about what learning strategies the students can use for this task. We agree that we will make a model together and that the students will then work in groups to brainstorm for their own first practice draft. We also agree that they will edit each other's work. But everyone agrees that it is a good idea to have a simulated essay exam after they have practiced so that they can experience what the actual exam will be like.

- Planning ahead: It is time to go into Week 2 and prepare several drafts. To be ready for this work, the students write in their journals again. Now that the students have looked at what they know about autobiography and the writing process and what the writing prompt will be like, they will benefit from writing down their ideas about how they will prepare. They have about 15 minutes to write, and I read and react to their entries.

Activities, Week 2: Producing Drafts

Writing is hard work. If ESOL students are honest with themselves and with their teachers, they will say that writing is not their favorite activity, but if they have structure and know what they are supposed to do, if they have good models, if they can work together on the task, and if they have class time to get started and to ask questions, they are more willing to work at the task, and they are happier with what they produce.

Even in a class of students who are supposedly at the same level, there is a spread from inexpert to quite competent writers. Students should not feel that they are competing with other writers in the class or, especially, with the professional writers they read. Some students will do well to follow instructions and a model and produce something that looks like an essay. Other students are advanced enough to produce something quite original and distinct from the usual models. I encourage all students to start where they are, do their best work, and be proud of their own progress.

Most students have less trouble producing a draft if they can do so on a computer. However, for this exam they have to write out their draft by hand. I remind students that they want to make their work as easy as possible for the readers, so they should use their best handwriting, leave margins, and make their work look inviting on the page. This is easier for some students than for others.

There is always the question of whether to focus on vocabulary and grammar and whether to allow the students to use dictionaries. These are areas that the students should have been working on all along in their ESL studies. It is outside the scope of this unit to talk about these issues at length, but teachers may want to do some practice with the dictionary as the students are producing their drafts and before they do the simulation and take the exam. Our classroom has ESL dictionaries, beginning-level English dictionaries, and the college edition of *The American Heritage Dictionary* (1991), all of which the students are allowed to use.

The best strategy that I have passed on to my students is one that I use when I write and that I think most writers use when they have to write on demand: If you cannot figure out how to spell the word or if you do not know if that is the right way to write a sentence, use a different word or a different way. Under these circumstances, it is better to have a simple sentence that is clear than a complicated one that is not.

Goal 2, Standard 2   To use English to achieve academically in all content areas: Students will use English to obtain, process, construct, and provide subject matter information in spoken and written form.

Descriptors

- listening to, speaking, reading, and writing about subject matter information
- gathering information orally and in writing
- selecting, connecting, and explaining information
- responding to the work of peers and others

Progress Indicators

- talk with peers about plans for writing an essay
- read drafts of peers and offer suggestions
- edit and revise own written assignments

Working Together to Get Started

Of the methods I have used to get students started, making a model as a class seems to work the best. Another possibility is to give students examples of student essays.

PROCEDURE

- Reviewing the prompt: I ask the students to take out the writing prompt that I have given them. We review what it means and what it is asking for. Then I explain that we are going to produce a class essay together. The students have the option of copying what I am writing on the board or just watching and helping. I ask one student to be the class secretary and copy what is put on the board.

- Organizing the model essay: The students give ideas right away, and the brainstorming web grows quickly on the board. Then we organize the ideas by finding an incident to focus on. We circle the phrases in the web that will help us. We erase the board and write just those items that have to do with our incident. We refine our organization by putting the items in order for the essay and adding other actions and details that we need.

- Writing pieces of the essay: I ask the students to take out their clock of partners. As I explain the next step, I write it on the board: Each pair will be assigned the beginning, the middle, or the end of the essay. The pairs will have about 15 minutes to produce a sketchy first draft of that section of the essay. Then I tell them which partner to go to and which section to work on.

- Following up: When the class comes back together, we read and discuss what different groups have done. Obviously, the results are a little disjointed, but the students get the idea. For homework, I assign brainstorming for an incident they will write on individually the next day.

Producing a First Draft

The students write the first draft of their individual essays in class.

PROCEDURE

- Using homework: The students return the next day with their brainstorming. They work in pairs talking about what they have and how to organize it.

- Getting started: I give them some time to work on their first draft in class to get them started. The draft is due in 2 days. We devote some time in class each day for the students to work on their drafts and discuss their work.

Editing: Self, Peer, Teacher

On the day the drafts are due, I stamp them with my draft stamp and pair students by pulling out two drafts and asking those two students to work together. Peer editing is very important, but it is intimidating for many students, so I give specific instructions.

PROCEDURE

- Pairing instructions: Before I pair the students, I review the peer editing procedure. First, they are to be positive in their responses, looking for what is good and giving suggestions for making the writing better. One person reads the other person's paper aloud in a quiet voice. They make changes in words that the reader cannot read or understand.

- Focused review: After they read the draft, they look for a specific list of items:

    1. What is the incident?
    2. Is there a beginning, a middle, and an end?
    3. Does the writer use good details?
    4. Does the writer use dialogue?
    5. Does the writer use complete sentences?

    When they finish with one paper, they work on the other one. I give them about 17 minutes to complete this task. If they finish early, they can check spelling and sentence structure, and they can begin reworking the drafts based on the suggestions made. The reworked draft is due the next day.

- Individual conferencing: While these pairs are working, I call the few students who did not hand in a draft to the front of the room near the board. We work on an incident together. Their assignment is to complete this incident for the next day.

- Assessment: The next day I ask for questions, have the students staple together their brainstorming and the first and second drafts of their papers, and collect the papers. I go over them out of class, writing suggestions and telling the students what is strong in their writing and what they still need to work on. In this assignment, the purpose is not to produce a perfect ready-to-publish copy but to be prepared to write a good first draft in a timed situation. Therefore, they can make a final draft of their paper if they wish and hand it in for extra credit. In class we talk about how to condense the writing process enough to allow them to write a good first draft alone and in one sitting.

Activities, Week 3: Taking the Exam

As I mentioned at the beginning of this unit, my purpose is not primarily to prepare the students for this exam. It is to show them how much they know about writing and how they can adapt what they know to specific situations; however, the students really want to do well on the exam. Therefore, the students take a simulated essay exam a few days before the real exam. Note that the descriptor and progress indicators here are from San Mateo Union High School District (1997) rather than from TESOL's (1997) ESL standards.

Goal 2, Standard 2   To use English to achieve academically in all content areas: Students will use English to obtain, process, construct, and provide subject matter information in spoken and written form.

Descriptor

- use a writing prompt to guide the development of a piece of writing

Progress Indicators

- produce a draft of an autobiographical incident that shows emotions and character through dialogue and action
- produce a good first draft of an autobiographical incident in a timed situation

---

Simulated Essay Exam

The more practice that students have for important exams and timed writing situations, the more comfortable they are when the real day comes. It is important for the students to understand the concept and purpose of simulation before engaging in one.

PROCEDURE

- Simulation: I explain what a simulation is. The students come to class as if it were the exam day. I give the instructions as I will on the test day, reading the prompt with them, showing them the special paper they need to use, and reminding them that they can use dictionaries. They write their essays.

- Assessment: When they finish, they turn in all of their scratch paper and the draft, stapled to the writing prompt. That night I read the drafts and score them as they will be scored by the district. The next day I share them with the students, being careful to point out that although I have been a part of the district scoring team and am fairly confident of my scoring, one never knows how other scorers will react. I give them points for their simulated essay based on their effort. As Monica's essay shows, she is ready to write about an autobiographical incident.

- A look ahead: We share tips for doing the best job possible on the exam day.

Monica's Essay

Once I thought I was lost. That day my mother told us that she had to do same shopping in a market near our house. My mother was wearing a wonderful red dress that she never had used before till that day.

In the moment that my mom was ready she called us "Come on Mony and Helen. Are you ready?" I was very impatient that I didn't care if I was ready or not. So when we were almost getting to the market I stopped at a wonderful school near the market, but I didn't see if my mom was with me or not. When I looked for her, unfortunate she wasn't there with me. First I stayed there for about five minutes wishing that my mom looked for me. By that moment I saw that a beautiful woman was passing with a little girl, but I didn't recognize her. So I got nervious and I went to the market and asked if anybody saw my mom, but nobody know were my

continued on p. 124

mom was. I remembered that before we went out of my house my mother told me "If we get time after we buy all our things for dinner. We can go to visit your aunt Juana." So I ran through the store were my aunt was and I told her all that was happening to me. My aunt Juana told me "You shall stay here with me and if your mom doesn't come. I'll go with you to your house." So after that I saw the beautiful woman with a wonderful red dress again. When she got close to us I saw that she was my mother and I was so happy that I wasn't really lost. I said to her "I'm so sorry that I'll never do it again."

Now I'm so happy that I wasn't lost. I learnr that all the kids in the world have to be sure that their mothers are with them in all the moments. when they go out because they can be lost. and never saw their families again.

Essay Competency Exam

We are back where we started from in this unit, with 24 students confidently taking the District Essay Competency Exam. A number of students will pass the exam, but the real success is that through this unit the students have learned how to write to a prompt. They have learned how to apply their knowledge of writing and autobiography to a different situation.

RESOURCES AND REFERENCES

Classroom Resources

The American heritage dictionary. (1991). Boston: Houghton Mifflin.
> *There are many good dictionaries, but my students and I like this one because the definitions and examples are clear and easy to work with. In addition, the dictionary's usage panel takes on some thorny questions, which are presented clearly with the appropriate entries. The illustrations and the biographical and geographical sections are also helpful.*

Boley, T., Golub, J. N., & McBride, W. L. (1997). *The language of literature: Blue level.* Evanston, IL: McDougal Littell.
> *This book is excellent for ESOL students who will soon be mainstreamed. It is full of fiction, nonfiction, poetry, and drama arranged in units by themes. It is also an excellent backup for teaching about writing and grammar and for analyzing literature. It is richly illustrated with art and realia and includes short biographies of the authors. Excerpts from* The Autobiography of Malcolm X, The Autobiography of Eleanor Roosevelt, *and W. J. Jacobs' biography of Eleanor Roosevelt are all in this volume.*

Cisneros, S. (1984). *The house on Mango Street.* New York: Vintage Books.
> *This book has already become a classic. Esperanza Cordero, the narrator, takes the reader with her into the scary territory of growing up. The first time I used this book, I was worried that the boys would see it as a girls' book, but that is not so. In addition to being a wonderful piece of first-person writing, the book is an excellent introduction to poetry and metaphoric language.*

Collins, D. R. (1996). *Farmworkers' friend: The story of Cesar Chavez.* Minneapolis, MN: Carolrhoda Books.
> *This excellent, short, illustrated biography of Chavez is easy to read and has a good bibliography.*

Freedman, R. (1993). *Eleanor Roosevelt: A life of discovery.* New York: Scholastic Books.
> *This illustrated biography is inspirational and well written. Each chapter opens with a quote from Roosevelt. The focus is clearly on her own life, but because her family was such an important part of her life, there is much good information about her husband and children.*

Hesse, K. (1992). *Letters from Rifka.* New York: Puffin Books.
> *The author's note explains how Hesse's desire to write about her family's migration from Russia to the United States led her to correspond with her great-aunt Lucy and interview her in person. Based on Aunt Lucy's stories, this wonderful book consists of letters from Rifka to her cousin Tovah as she makes her way to join her family in the United States.*

Lord, B. B. (1984). *In the year of the boar and Jackie Robinson.* New York: HarperTrophy.
> *Lord's adult books draw on her own life and family in China. This short book for young people is based on her own experience as a child moving from China to Brooklyn, and the connection between her struggle to make a new life for herself in the United States and Jackie Robinson's struggle to desegregate professional baseball.*

Martinez, V. (1996). *Parrot in the oven: Mi vida.* New York: HarperTrophy.
> *This National Book Award winner is based on Martinez's own childhood in Fresno, California. Life is not easy for Manny Hernandez and his family, but it is funny, human, and very touching.*

Soto, G. (1985). *Living up the street.* New York: Bantam Doubleday Dell Books.
> *Poet and young people's author Soto uses his childhood in Fresno, California, as the basis for a number of books. His prose is poetry, and it is very funny. He makes everyday problems into adventures and lessons about life.*

Thorndike, E. L., & Barnhart, C. L. *Scott, Foresman beginning dictionary.* (1979). Glenview, IL: Scott, Foresman.
> *This dictionary is intended for elementary school students, but it is very useful as a step beyond bilingual dictionaries for my students. They get used to working with definitions in English rather than translations and learn how to work with an English dictionary. Even after they have graduated to* The American Heritage Dictionary, *they still come back to the Scott, Foresman Beginning Dictionary for clarification. They do not feel talked down to at all by this book.*

Uchida, Y. (1978). *Journey home.* New York: Aladdin Paperbacks/Simon & Schuster.
> *When my older daughter was in fourth grade, she brought me a book called* A Jar of Dreams *and told me that she knew I would love it. I did, and my students and I have loved everything that Uchida has written for children and adults. This book is based on her experiences in the U.S. concentration camp Topaz. Her stories are always realistic and hopeful.*

Teacher References

Celce-Murcia, M., & Larsen-Freeman, D. (1999). *The grammar book: An ESL/EFL teacher's course* (2nd ed.). Boston: Heinle & Heinle.
> *This invaluable resource for ESL teachers contains explanations and teaching suggestions for almost any grammatical question you might run into.*

Chamot, A. U., Barnhardt, S., El-Dinary, P. B., & Robbins, J. (1999). *The learning strategies handbook.* White Plains, NY: Addison Wesley Longman.
> *This handbook is full of activities and evaluation ideas that get ESOL students involved and thinking.*

Chamot, A. U., & O'Malley, J. M. (1994). *The CALLA handbook: Implementing the cognitive academic language learning approach.* Reading, MA: Addison-Wesley.
> *This very practical book is full of ideas and activities that include learning strategies. There are sections on science, mathematics, social studies, and literature and composition. The last section has been very useful in planning literature and writing activities for my students.*

O'Malley, J. M., & Pierce, L. V. (1996). *Authentic assessment for English language learners: Practical approaches for teachers.* Reading, MA: Addison-Wesley.
> *This handbook includes many ideas for assessment for K–12 ESL teachers. There are checklists, rubrics, self-evaluations, and much more.*

Peitzman, F., & Gadda, G. (Eds.). (1994). *With different eyes: Insights into teaching language minority students across the disciplines.* White Plains, NY: Longman.
> *This collection of articles came out of the University of California at Los Angeles's writing program. The authors are university and high school professionals concerned about helping minority students make a successful transition from high school to college. Both the literature and writing suggestions are excellent.*

San Mateo Union High School District. (1997, February). *Master plan for English-as-a-second-language.* (Available from San Mateo Union High School District, 650 North Delaware Street, San Mateo, CA 94401)
> *The ESL department chairs and other ESL teachers worked on a task force to prepare this document, which gives the mission, goals, levels, standards, exit criteria at each level and for each standard, and course outlines for the core ESL courses. In addition to their own experience, the task force drew on TESOL's (1997) Pre-K–12 standards and various state and district documents in preparing this plan.*

TESOL. (1997). *ESL standards for Pre-K–12 students.* Alexandria, VA: Author.

TESOL. (in press). *Scenarios for ESL standards-based assessment.* Alexandria, VA: Author.

UNIT 6
Creating a Community of Social Studies Learners

ELLEN DANIELS *and* GEORGE C. BUNCH

Introduction

How do we address the language needs of our students while covering the content curriculum?

How do we share ideas with colleagues when we are the only ones at our schools who teach a particular class?

How do inexperienced teachers find ways to meet the demands of complex classrooms?

How do we use alternative assessment techniques while preparing students for standardized tests?

How do we help prepare ESOL students to pass the upcoming state history assessments required for graduation?

How do we teach the entire history of the United States in 1 year to students who have never heard of George Washington?

How do we communicate better with mainstream social studies departments to ensure that our students are included in the overall high school academic program?

What are these new ESL standards, and what are we supposed to do with them?

Several years ago, these were the questions that George, a first-year ESL content-area teacher, was pondering when he met Ellen, a third-year ESL content-area teacher at a

---

Context

Grade levels: 9th–12th grades

English proficiency levels: Beginning–advanced

Native languages of students: 18 languages, including Spanish, Korean, Chinese, and Vietnamese

Focus of instruction: U.S. history

Type of class: Sheltered content

Length of unit: 3 weeks

different high school in the same school district. She had been mulling over the same questions. Today, we are still exploring the questions and grappling with answers.

Early in our collaboration, we discovered the power of simply talking to each other about our questions. We realized that, although we come into contact with hundreds of people a day in our schools, we were also working in isolation. In a professional world with so many demands on people's time, we noticed that collaboration was not something that occurred naturally.

We started our collaboration rather informally. George visited Ellen's school one day in the middle of the school year as part of his ongoing new-teacher orientation. That visit led to sharing materials and ideas, which led to occasional e-mail exchanges. Although this early communication was not structured, it was valuable in that it gave us an opportunity to continue to discuss our questions, share successes, and troubleshoot problems.

Our collaboration became more structured when we decided to cofacilitate a discussion group on teaching secondary social studies at the local TESOL affiliate's convention. Deciding to continue the discussion on a larger scale, we led a similar session at the 33rd Annual TESOL Convention in New York in 1999. Not surprisingly, many of our original questions were on the minds of our colleagues around the country.

When our school district distributed copies of *ESL Standards for Pre-K–12 Students* (TESOL, 1997) to all ESL teachers, we found that the same time constraints that limit professional collaboration also limited our ability to process the new information and integrate it into our teaching practice. Writing this chapter has given us the opportunity not only to process the standards but also to find ways to use them in addressing our questions. At the same time, this project has allowed us to continue collaboration in order to create a structure for more effective lesson planning. Most important, we can now expand our collaboration by sharing what we have learned with others.

We teach U.S. history to ESOL students at different high schools about 1 mile apart in a diverse suburb near Washington, DC. As a result of our schools' geographic proximity, our teaching contexts are similar. At both schools, mainstream and ESOL populations are linguistically and culturally diverse. We both teach classes containing students at a mix of English proficiency levels. Our students come from a wide range of academic backgrounds, including students whose education was interrupted or who are otherwise underprepared academically. A large majority of our students receive free or reduced-price meals, a common indication of poverty. This chapter reflects components from each of our classes.

Unit Overview

Education involves a dynamic interaction between what to learn and how to learn it. In the ESL social studies classroom, "what to learn" includes content, language, and academic skills. At the same time, the sheltered-content classroom is an important place for students to explore "how to learn." Although these two strands are necessarily intertwined, we divide them below in order to address them in detail and to correlate the skills involved in each part with the ESL standards. For this unit, the strand involving what to learn includes selected content, language, and social studies skills needed for the study of the Great Depression. Because this unit serves as a planning template that could be used with any social studies content, this strand includes only a few of the activities that we would actually do in teaching a unit on the Great Depression. The strand involving how to learn explains the conscious development of a community of learners.

Strand 1: The Great Depression

"The Great Depression" is one unit of our district's U.S. history curriculum. Because this course is the credit-bearing U.S. history course that is required for high school graduation, we begin the planning process with the instructional and performance objectives from our school system's mainstream curriculum.

The instructional objective is to explain the causes and effects of the Great Depression. The performance objectives are to

- explain the factors that caused the Great Depression
- evaluate the steps that President Hoover took to restore prosperity
- describe the programs that implemented FDR's New Deal policy
- describe the economic effects of the Great Depression on American society
- evaluate the achievements of the New Deal (Montgomery County Public Schools, 1992)

The unit overview on the next page shows the planning process we use; we write our objectives in terms of things students should be able to do upon completing the unit.

Our next step is to integrate these objectives into a theme in order to pique the interest of the students and relate the content to their personal experiences. We introduce themes and guide the students to explore them through a set of essential questions for each unit. The questions are purposefully broad, intended to promote discussion rather than to elicit definitive answers.

We introduce essential questions at the beginning of each unit using a variety of methods, which vary with the content of the questions and the students in the class. Usually, we begin by discussing new vocabulary and concepts in the questions themselves. Next, we may lead a whole-class discussion, conduct a **think/pair/share** activity, or simply challenge the students to think about the questions as we continue to study the unit. We revisit the questions at appropriate times throughout the unit, encouraging the students to consider them in light of new material that we encounter. If time allows, they can record their new reflections in a journal, or share ideas with a partner or small group. We review the essential questions at the end of the unit as a means of closure.

For this unit on the Great Depression, we chose the following essential questions because we thought they particularly addressed the social reality of many of our students:

1. What are the effects of poverty and unemployment on society?
2. What is the role of government in solving society's problems?

After considering the unit objectives and the essential questions (what to learn) in order to address the academic needs of our students, we turned to the equally important topic of meeting those needs (how to learn).

Strand 2: Creating a Community of Learners

Needless to say, for ESOL students, the academic demands of meeting the unit objectives are great. As sheltered content teachers, we need to find means of helping our students bridge the gap between their academic backgrounds and the new curricular demands of the U.S. school system. We believe that students cannot cross this bridge individually. Rather, we search for ways to help them work together in confronting challenging academic situations. Through cooperative learning, students have the opportunity to interact with each other as well as with the content material.

Unit Overview: Creating a Community of Social Studies Learners

Unit _____

Unit Title: _____

Essential Question(s):

Unit Introduction

- Activate background knowledge
- Discuss essential questions
- Preview instructional and performance objectives

MCPS instructional objective(s): _____

Language objective(s): _____

[Repeat this box for each performance objective.]

Performance objective: _____	TESOL standards
- Activate background knowledge - Preview objectives and lesson plan - Deliver content/teach skill - Practice and apply - Evaluate: formally and informally - Expand: link to current events and personal lives	[integrated into lesson]

Unit Conclusion

- Final project
- Discussion of essential questions
- Review of instructional and performance objectives
- Review of lessons
- Final exam
- Expansion

One of our central goals in teaching is to establish a comfortable atmosphere in our classrooms, where students trust and respect one another enough to take the risks necessary for learning. Such an atmosphere promotes learning in our own classrooms and helps the students develop the skills necessary for success in mainstream classrooms. This goal does not come naturally or easily. At times it may even seem impossible. The key is to build instruction in such a way that all classroom participants know the goal explicitly and are given the tools with which to achieve this goal.

Cooperative learning also provides an opportunity to practice social skills in the classroom and create an atmosphere of trust and respect. In a multicultural classroom, working in groups gives students exposure to different norms in communication. With explicit skill instruction and guidance, students can learn how to deal with these differences and how to express themselves in a manner appropriate to the setting.

Another function of cooperative learning is to help students acquire the skills they need to survive in mainstream content classrooms. Many of these skills are academic, preparing students to meet the challenges of rigorous materials and high expectations. But our students also need social and cultural awareness to interact successfully with their mainstream peers. Moving into a mainstream class can be an overwhelming experience for an ESOL student. Students have often expressed that their greatest fear is not whether they will be able to pass the class (although this is certainly a preoccupation of theirs!) but whether they will be teased or excluded by their peers.

Although we have separated Strand 1 (The Great Depression) and Strand 2 (Creating a Community of Learners) in this description for the purpose of explanation, we note that in the planning of a unit it is important to consider both simultaneously. This presented a challenge. We were looking for a systematic way to plan a unit that would help make the district curriculum accessible to ESOL students and foster the growth of a community of learners. We looked to the ESL standards (TESOL, 1997) for guidance.

Standards

As ESL social studies teachers, our continuing struggle is to balance the language and content needs of our students. Before the ESL standards were developed, our only explicit guidance came from two sources: (a) the district curriculum, which was designed for mainstream students and included few accommodations for students with special needs, and (b) ESL social studies and U.S. history textbooks, which did not adequately address the district curriculum objectives. What was missing were guidelines and resources for facilitating ESOL students' access to the rigorous academic content expected by our school system.

The ESL standards helped fill that void. The standards were designed, in part, to "provide the bridge to general education standards expected of all students in the United States" (TESOL, 1997, p. 2). In fact, one of the three goals is devoted exclusively to content-area academic achievement. The standards articulate the language competencies our students need to be successful in content classes.

We explored ways to integrate the ESL standards with the district curriculum objectives in a format that would facilitate our planning for each unit. As a result, we created a unit chart that combines the ESL standards and district objectives with our own essential questions, specific language objectives, effective teaching methods, appropriate assessments, and time guidelines. We designed the chart using reflections on our own experiences and literature on content-based ESL instruction (e.g., Brinton & Masters, 1997; Chamot & O'Malley, 1994; Crandall, 1987; Short, 1991). See the Additional Information section at the end of this chapter for selections from the chart and an explanation of how to use it.

Because our primary concern is how to provide challenging and complex content to ESOL high school students, we begin below by describing several unit activities in terms of how they address Goal 2 of the ESL standards (to use English to achieve academically in all content areas). Subsequently, we describe our approach to implementing cooperative learning in terms of how it addresses Goal 1 (to use English to communicate in social settings) and Goal 3 (to use English in socially and culturally appropriate ways).

While working with the ESL standards to plan our unit, we found that more than one standard applies to each individual activity. For each standard that we address, therefore, we choose an activity that we believe illustrates well the essence of that standard. We have selected three content-related activities to explain in more detail in Strand 1 below. The unit chart at the end of this chapter delineates how these activities interrelate with the rest of the unit.

Each of the activities we have chosen, however, could be reframed to illustrate a completely different standard. The sample pages from our unit chart (see the Additional Information section, pp. 146–148) show how different standards can apply to each activity. This material shows the relationships between the activities and the standards and among the standards themselves. It also illustrates the multidimensional aspect of teaching—how the classroom always integrates social, academic, and cultural activity.

Activities, Strand 1: Learning Social Studies Content

Discovery Learning Activity

In this activity, student groups extract specific causes of the Great Depression from their textbook, summarize them, and present them to the class. Each group is responsible for a separate cause. By sharing information, all the students end up with a complete outline of targeted information. This activity provides a student-centered means of encountering new content, an opportunity to practice reading skills, and the benefit of working in a group with students who have a variety of abilities. By this point in the school year, the students have been introduced to and have practiced the individual skills involved in reading for specific information, summarizing, and presenting to a large group.

Depending on the needs of the students, the texts available, and the content goals of the lesson, we use either a single text for the entire class, different texts for each group, or different texts for each member of a group. The advantage of using one text for the entire class is that we can guide the class as each group presents so that other students can understand how and where they found the information. If one text is not adequate for covering the content desired, or if we want to accommodate groups of different reading levels, we might use a different text for each group. Using different texts within each group makes it possible to compare authors' perspectives, pool information on a topic, or accommodate students of different reading levels.

Cooperation and communication are necessary at various levels during this activity. The students need to interact with their peers in a small group to complete a task that is essential for the entire class. The students also need to present their work to a group coherently and be prepared for potential questions from the class.

Procedure

- Before beginning the activity, we pose questions to the students to activate their background knowledge. To connect with their personal experiences, we ask them, "Do you know someone who is unemployed?" and "Why do people lose their jobs?" To tap into prior learning in this course, we ask the students to describe the U.S. economy in the 1920s and talk about the economic risks people took. The students have 5 minutes to do a **quickwrite** on the topic, followed by a brief class discussion.

Goal 2, Standard 1 To use English to achieve academically in all content areas: Students will use English to interact in the classroom.

Descriptors

- following oral and written directions, implicit and explicit
- participating in full-class, group, and pair discussions
- negotiating and managing interaction to accomplish tasks

Progress Indicators

- follow directions to form groups
- negotiate cooperative roles in task assignments
- negotiate verbally to identify roles in preparation for a group/class presentation

- To prepare for the activity, the students preview the text by examining titles, headings, and graphics.

- To begin, we divide the students into groups. Each group receives a different key word or phrase, such as *farm problems* or *weak banking system,* to locate in their textbook. Their task is to summarize pertinent information and present it to the class. At the same time, the groups identify key content vocabulary that they have encountered.

*Throughout the year we encourage the students to identify unknown vocabulary in given texts. With the students, we make a comprehensive list of words to study for that unit, which we display on a **word wall**. We add essential vocabulary the students have missed and delete words not directly relevant to the content of the unit; we may practice the deleted words in other contexts, but they do not become part of the target vocabulary list. We hope that participating in the construction of the word list will motivate the students to learn the meanings of the words.*

- In each group, each student assumes a different role: timekeeper, information recorder, vocabulary recorder, and spokesperson.

- When the groups are finished collecting the data, spokespersons from each group present their findings. The students record all information presented in outline form, facilitated by the teacher.

- The students write in their journals, explaining what they believe to be the most important causes of the Great Depression.

Assessment

While the groups collect information, we observe the students participating in their groups, taking note of how they interact and contribute to their group's effort. In addition, the students are given checklists, such as the one shown on the next page, to assess their group's behavior. We read journal entries to check on the students' comprehension.

Cooperative Group Checklist		
I helped my group complete the task.	Yes	No
I listened to other students in my group.	Yes	No
I was polite to other members of my group.	Yes	No
We summarized our topic.	Yes	No
We found three vocabulary words.	Yes	No

"You're the Historian!"

One of the social studies skills we teach is how to read primary sources. In this activity, we challenge the students to be actual historians. The students learn about the policies of Herbert Hoover and his response to the economic crisis at the start of the Great Depression, and use their knowledge about Hoover to hypothesize which of a list of quotations could be attributed to him. They return to the other quotations later in this unit after a lesson on Franklin D. Roosevelt.

Goal 2, Standard 2 To use English to achieve academically in all content areas: Students will use English to obtain, process, construct, and provide subject matter information in spoken and written form.

Descriptors

- comparing and contrasting information
- selecting, connecting, and explaining information
- analyzing, synthesizing, and inferring from information
- hypothesizing and predicting
- demonstrating knowledge through application in a variety of contexts

Progress Indicators

- synthesize, analyze, and evaluate information
- take a position and support it orally or in writing
- use contextual clues

PROCEDURE

- To help the students recall information learned in the previous lesson, they complete a think/pair/share activity based on journal entries they wrote during the previous lesson evaluating the causes of the Great Depression.
- The students do two tasks to ensure that they learn the necessary content before the following quotation activity. First, they complete reading charts

that show increasing unemployment and declining wages in the early 1930s. Second, we present a minilecture covering Hoover's response to the economic problems facing the United States, and the students create an outline of the information in their notebooks.

- We tell the students to imagine that they are professional historians who have been asked to help clarify which of a variety of statements were likely to have been made by President Hoover. We remind the students to use what they know about Hoover's policies to complete the task.

- We give each student a list of quotations by Hoover and Roosevelt (shown on the next page). After reading each quotation and discussing problematic vocabulary as a class, the students write "Hoover" next to the quotations they believe represent his policy.

- The students compare their lists with a partner's, discussing why they chose the quotations they did and trying to come to a consensus on quotations that are in dispute.

- We have volunteers read each quotation, recording a tally of "votes" for Hoover next to each quotation and discussing with the class why the quotation might or might not represent his philosophy. We then reveal the correct answer.

- After a review of the grammatical conventions of quoted and reported speech, the students individually complete an activity in which they change Hoover's quotations into reported speech (e.g., *Hoover said that* _____).

> Throughout the course, we discuss what professional historians do and help the students realize that they are learning and practicing real-life skills (e.g., using and understanding the differences between primary and secondary sources, determining causes and effects of historical events, using historical clues to hypothesize about missing information, linking past events with present-day realities). If the activities are engaging, the students enjoy them and are empowered by knowing they are real historians.

Assessment

We assess the students' performance by observing their discussions with partners, analyzing the arguments they present to the class, and correcting the grammar activity. A generic instrument for assessing cooperative learning activities is given on page 144. For more examples of designing checklists for specific activities, see *Scenarios for ESL Standards-Based Assessment* (TESOL, in press). As a follow-up activity in the next lesson, students revisit the list of quotations after being introduced to Franklin D. Roosevelt, as a way to better understand the election of 1932 and some of the fundamental differences between the Republican and Democratic parties.

> "Presidential Quotations" can be adapted for lower level students by rewriting the quotations in simpler English. Likewise, more advanced students can be challenged by additional, more difficult quotations.

___

Presidential Quotations

The following words were spoken by either President Hoover or President Roosevelt between 1928 and 1933. Based on what you have learned about President Hoover, decide which quotations you think he said and write "Hoover" on the line after the quotation.

1. "We in America are nearer to the final triumph over poverty than ever before in the history of any land. Given a chance to go forward with the policies of the last eight years, we shall soon with the help of God be in the sight of the day when poverty will be banished from this nation." _____

2. "Our greatest primary task is to put people to work. This is no unsolvable problem if we face it wisely and courageously." _____

3. "This nation asks for action, and action now." _____

4. "The fundamental business of the country is on a sound and prosperous basis."_____

5. "We have now passed the worst and shall rapidly recover." _____

6. "Economic depression cannot be cured by legislative action or executive pronouncement. The best contribution of government lies in encouragement of this voluntary cooperation in the community." _____

7. "Taxes have risen; our ability to pay has fallen; . . . farmers find no markets for their produce; the savings of many years in thousands of families are gone." _____

8. "I shall ask Congress for . . . broad executive power to wage a war against the [economic] emergency as great as the power that would be given me if we were in fact invaded by a foreign foe." _____

Sources: Nos. 2, 3, 7, and 8, Hyser and Arndt (1995, pp. 160–162); Nos. 1 and 4–6, Montgomery County Public Schools (1992, pp. x–31).

___

Final Project: New Deal Programs That Are Alive Today

The culminating activity of this unit is a project that connects the information learned about the programs of the New Deal to real-life experience. In this way, the students learn to view history not simply as something that happened in the past and no longer exists but as a dynamic influence on people's lives today. Students find more meaning in what they have learned if they can understand its contemporary relevance.

Using current resources can be a challenge for ESOL students. In this activity, the students must learn to use a variety of learning strategies for approaching unknown texts.

PROCEDURE

- To link the final project to the students' background knowledge, we guide them to recall the New Deal programs that they have learned about in this unit. The students quickly brainstorm several programs, and we record them on the blackboard.

Goal 2, Standard 3 To use English to achieve academically in all content areas: Students will use appropriate learning strategies to construct and apply academic knowledge.

Descriptors

- focusing attention selectively
- applying basic reading comprehension skills such as skimming, scanning, previewing, and reviewing text
- taking notes to record important information and aid one's own learning
- planning how and when to use cognitive strategies and applying them appropriately to a learning task
- actively connecting new information to information previously learned

Progress Indicators

- make predictions
- scan several resources to determine the appropriateness to the topic of study
- take notes to summarize the main points provided in source material
- verbalize relationships between new information and information previously learned in another setting
- select materials from school resource collections to complete a project

- We ask the students to predict which programs might still exist today. The students volunteer their hypotheses, within the established classroom expectation that all answers are equally valid as long as they are reasonably explained and based on prior learning.

- We tell the students that they will get a list of several programs that originated during the New Deal era and still exist today. Before distributing this list, we remind the students of one of the essential questions of the unit: "What is the role of government in solving society's problems?" We suggest that the students keep this question in mind while conducting their research.

- We distribute the list of New Deal programs alive today, such as Social Security, the Securities and Exchange Commission, and the Federal Deposit Insurance Corporation, and ask the students to choose one of interest.

> Prediction is a learning strategy that prepares students for encounters with new material. It allows them to reflect on what they know and prepares their minds to approach related information. Whether their predictions are correct or incorrect is not important; what is important is that they create their own mental links to the topic and, in so doing, become interested in finding more information.

- The students create a plan for the research that they will conduct in the media center the next day:

    1. We give them the "Research Project Planning Worksheet" below and ask them to fill it out with pertinent information about their research plans (i.e., the title of their New Deal program and specific predictions about who may be helped by this particular program today).

    2. The students choose and prioritize three of a variety of listed sources (e.g., newspapers, magazines, on-line and print encyclopedias, World Wide Web sites) in which to find information about their topic.

    3. We explicitly direct students of different proficiency levels to specific resources. For example, CD-ROM encyclopedias may be more accessible for low-level students than the Internet sites of major

> We want the essential questions to motivate the students. By revisiting these questions, the students can build on their prior knowledge and integrate new material as they progress through the unit.

Research Project Planning Worksheet

Project title: _____

Predictions:

Sources (choose three and prioritize):

Newspaper sources:　　____　_____

　　　　　　　　　　　　____　_____

____　other newspaper source: _____

Magazine sources:　　____　_____

　　　　　　　　　　　　____　_____

____　other magazine source: _____

Encyclopedia sources:　　____　_____

　　　　　　　　　　　　____　_____

____　other encyclopedia source: _____

CD-ROM sources:　　____　_____

　　　　　　　　　　　　____　_____

____　other CD-ROM source: _____

Internet sources:　　____　_____

　　　　　　　　　　　　____　_____

____　other Internet source: _____

newspapers and magazines. Students with very low proficiency or limited previous education can analyze pictures or graphs pertaining to the topic from a variety of sources.

- Before going to the media center, we review the process of note-taking as a class. We model examples of good notes to the students and review the strategy of scanning text for specific information. The students then examine examples of inappropriate notes (e.g., wordy notes, notes obviously copied from the text) and give suggestions on how to improve them. Finally, the students work in small groups to take notes from a short paragraph in order to practice the strategy.

- The class spends the next two class periods conducting research in the school's media center. Some students feel more comfortable with print sources and choose current magazines or newspapers on the shelves. Other students enjoy using computers and take advantage of any opportunity to go on-line. The students take notes on their topics.

- After the students complete their research, we conduct a minilesson on how to write a rough draft. The students begin their drafts in class and complete them for homework.

- The following day, the students meet in peer groups to edit each other's drafts using the "Peer Evaluation Checklist," reproduced on page 140. After everyone finishes peer editing, small groups conference about each report, pointing out the strengths of the work and highlighting areas for revision. The students discuss their suggestions with one another and plan the revisions for their final drafts.

- We review our expectations for the final copies with the students and distribute guidelines. The students have several days to complete their final copies at home.

Alternatively, low-proficiency students could buddy up with a more advanced student to complete the project. The student with lower English proficiency could be guided to illustrate or create graphs or charts for the final report. The vast resources of the Internet also provide the option of doing research in the students' native languages.

When working with the Internet, we bookmark a series of sites for the students to access quickly. In this way, we know at a glance if a student is in an appropriate site. It also saves time and keeps the students from getting lost in advertising.

ASSESSMENT

We assess the students using a rubric that incorporates the information from the "Peer Evaluation Checklist" (shown on the next page), the guidelines for the final copy, and the original task in the assessment process described above.

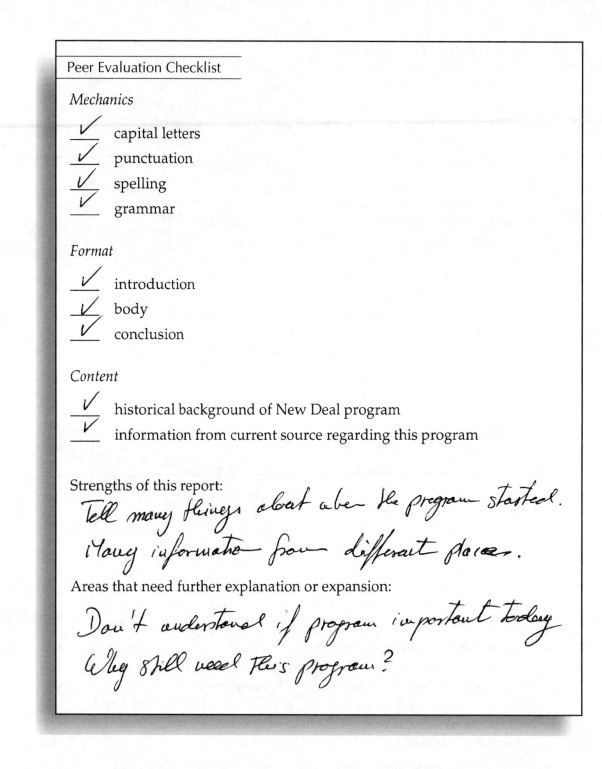

Peer Evaluation Checklist

Mechanics

- ✓ capital letters
- ✓ punctuation
- ✓ spelling
- ✓ grammar

Format

- ✓ introduction
- ✓ body
- ✓ conclusion

Content

- ✓ historical background of New Deal program
- ✓ information from current source regarding this program

Strengths of this report:

Tell many things about abe the program started.
Many informatio from different places.

Areas that need further explanation or expansion:

Don't understand if program important today
Why still need this program?

Activities, Strand 2: Cooperative Learning

As discussed earlier, cooperative learning is an integral part of our classroom instruction throughout this unit. As we examined the ESL standards, we realized that four standards correspond to almost every cooperative learning activity. Rather than addressing each of these standards within the context of the specific activities from this unit on the Great Depression, we instead describe the groundwork that we must lay at the beginning of the year to make all these activities successful.

In the preceding discovery learning activity, we address one standard related to cooperative learning: Goal 2, Standard 1 (to use English to achieve academically in all content areas: Students will use English to interact in the classroom). In this section, we address the other three standards that are closely linked with cooperative learning skills.

We begin each school year by discussing with the students three concepts that will lead to a successful year: learning, community, and respect. These concepts are reinforced throughout the year as the students develop cooperative learning skills. In conjunction with these concepts, another theme throughout the year is the importance of appropriate verbal and nonverbal communication with peers, especially when working in groups.

Depending on the purpose of the activity, we design either heterogeneous or homogeneous groups based on one or more of the following characteristics:

- language proficiency
- native language
- academic background
- learning styles
- gender
- personality
- motivation
- behavior

Students in heterogeneous groups can learn from each other, and homogeneous groups offer students opportunities to contribute in ways they might not in heterogeneous groups. What is important, we believe, is to use a variety of student groupings throughout the year to give students a range of experiences in working with others to develop a repertoire of skills.

We are aware of the culturally diverse ideas our students bring with them in regard to appropriate verbal and nonverbal communication, ways of interacting with peers, and other issues that may affect their level of comfort with what we ask them to do in the classroom. Our approach is twofold: We honor the students' cultural conceptions of communication and encourage them to discuss their traditions in class, and we model and encourage behavior we feel is expected of students in mainstream academic settings in the United States.

Viewing the Group as a Social Setting

Procedure

- Early in the year, we ask the students why they think we include so many group activities in the class. We also share our own beliefs with the students: Cooperative learning gives students the opportunity to know each other, to practice English, to learn what classmates think and feel about a variety of issues, and to prepare for mainstream classes and the working world.

- We allow the students to discuss their feelings about group activities. Students may not particularly like to work with others, and we respect that preference. Students need to know that they are still expected to participate in the activities and to try to do their best, but they also need to know that it is acceptable to prefer other kinds of activities and that they will have opportunities to learn individually at other times.

- Before the students leave their groups upon completing an activity, we remind them of the importance of thanking their peers.

Goal 1, Standard 1 To use English to communicate in social settings: Students will use English to participate in social interactions.

Descriptors

- sharing and requesting information
- expressing needs, feelings, and ideas
- using nonverbal communication in social interactions
- engaging in conversations

Progress Indicators

- defend and argue a position
- ask peers for their opinions, preferences, and desires
- engage listener's attention verbally or nonverbally
- elicit information and ask clarification questions
- offer and respond to greetings, compliments, invitations, introductions, and farewells
- negotiate solutions to problems, interpersonal misunderstandings, and disputes

Using Appropriate Language in Groups

Goal 3, Standard 1 To use English in socially and culturally appropriate ways: Students will use the appropriate language variety, register, and genre according to audience, purpose, and setting.

Descriptors

- using the appropriate degree of formality with different audiences and settings
- responding to and using slang appropriately
- responding to and using humor appropriately
- determining when it is appropriate to use a language other than English
- determining appropriate topics for interaction

Progress Indicators

- make polite requests
- use English and native languages appropriately in a multilingual social situation
- demonstrate an understanding of ways to give and receive compliments, show gratitude, apologize, express anger or impatience
- greet and take leave appropriately in a variety of settings

PROCEDURE

- We introduce target cooperative learning concepts by modeling them with role-plays as early in the year as possible. Because creating a community of learners skilled at working together in pairs and groups is an ongoing process, we incorporate reminders, feedback, and practice throughout the year.

- We address other topics on an ongoing basis. We discuss the appropriate use of humor, ways to encourage peers, and ways to deal with language misunderstandings. In addition, we discuss when it is helpful to use the native language and when it may be inappropriate. Finally, we discuss ways in which students may be able to help each other stay on task in an appropriate way.

Using Appropriate Nonverbal Communication in Groups

PROCEDURE

- At the beginning of the year, we model appropriate body language, such as making eye contact, and we suggest small-talk openings, such as "How's it going?" "Hot out, huh?" and "I'm tired; how about you?"

- We expect students to begin each group activity by shaking hands, greeting each other, introducing themselves or clarifying that they know each other's names, and engaging in small talk.

Goal 3, Standard 2 **To use English in socially and culturally appropriate ways: Students will use nonverbal communication appropriate to audience, purpose, and setting.**

Descriptors

- interpreting and responding appropriately to nonverbal cues and body language
- demonstrating knowledge of acceptable nonverbal classroom behaviors
- using acceptable tone, volume, stress, and intonation in various social settings
- recognizing and adjusting behavior in response to nonverbal cues

Progress Indicators

- advise peers on appropriate behaviors in and out of school
- determine the appropriate distance to maintain while working in a group
- maintain an appropriate level of eye contact while communicating with peers
- obtain a classmate's attention in an appropriate manner
- use the appropriate volume of voice while working with a group in a classroom

- Before the students start working in their groups, we encourage them to consider the type of activity they will be doing and the best way to arrange themselves. For example, two students working together and sharing a book should pull their desks next to one another. If four students are working cooperatively on an activity, they will need to form a circle so that they can all see each other. We discuss appropriate distances between group members and between groups.

- During the activities, we encourage the students to be mindful of our earlier discussions on appropriate and inappropriate verbal and nonverbal behavior.

- We conclude most cooperative activities with a time for each group to report its findings or results. During this reporting, spokespersons are asked to begin their presentation by introducing the other members of their group.

Cooperative Learning Activity Assessment										
Names										
Greeting										
On task										
Positive interaction										
Problem solving										
Asking questions										
Verbal communication										
Nonverbal communication										
Closure										
Comments										

ASSESSMENT

- When possible, at the end of a group activity we lead the students in a brief discussion about the benefits and challenges of completing the task with a group as opposed to individually.

- We use various checklists (such as the cooperative learning activity assessment shown here) as forms of self-, peer, and group evaluation. These can be focused on particular cooperative behaviors, content material, or presentation skills.

- Based on the information gathered in these assessments, we develop future minilessons on specific cooperative learning skills.

Cooperative learning clearly demonstrates the advantage of viewing assessment as having multiple phases within a unit. According to Scenarios for ESL Standards-Based Assessment (TESOL, in press), the assessment process has four phases: (a) planning assessments, (b) collecting and recording information, (c) analyzing and interpreting assessment information, and (d) using information for reporting and decision making. For us, this means that assessment is relevant not only for evaluating the students but also in planning instruction.

Additional Information: Unit Chart

The unit chart shown on the following pages provides a format for planning any unit for an ESL U.S. history course. It could be adapted for other content-area or language courses. The chart includes the essential questions and instructional and performance objectives plus three sections: (a) a unit introduction, (b) a page for each performance objective in the unit (because of space limitations, only one is included here), and (c) a unit conclusion. Each performance objective page outlines six steps:

- Activate background knowledge: When the unit is introduced, it is important for the students to connect the new topic to their previously developed schema. Appropriate activities include webs, brainstorming, quickwriting, think/pair/share, and class discussion.

- Preview objectives and lesson: This part of the unit gives the students their first exposure to new material. Here they learn what the overall plan is and where the lesson is headed, and engage in activities that make the content and text more accessible to the students. Appropriate activities include practicing prereading strategies (e.g., looking at the title and parts of the book, headings, and graphics) and beginning a K-W-L chart.

- Discover content/learn skill: Whether the teacher presents the core content to the students or the students encounter the information through a text or another source, the feeling of discovery for the student can be the goal of this part of the instruction. Appropriate activities include listening to a minilecture, taking notes, analyzing a primary source (e.g., letter, document, photo), analyzing a political cartoon, listening to a guest speaker, watching a video, learning a song, doing a discovery learning activity, interpreting graphs, reading literature, using the core text (with reading strategies), using an alternative text (with reading strategies), watching an interactive slide lecture, and making a word wall.

Unit Chart

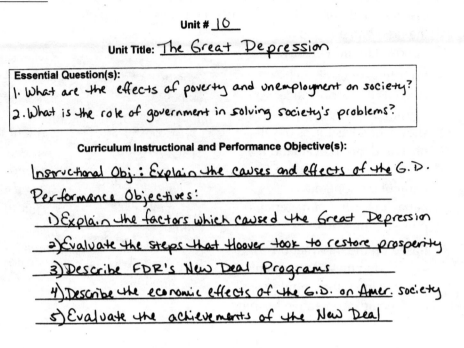

Unit # 10

Unit Title: The Great Depression

Essential Question(s):
1. What are the effects of poverty and unemployment on society?
2. What is the role of government in solving society's problems?

Curriculum Instructional and Performance Objective(s):

Instructional Obj.: Explain the causes and effects of the G.D.

Performance Objectives:

1) Explain the factors which caused the Great Depression

2) Evaluate the steps that Hoover took to restore prosperity

3) Describe FDR's New Deal Programs

4) Describe the economic effects of the G.D. on Amer. society

5) Evaluate the achievements of the New Deal

Unit Introduction

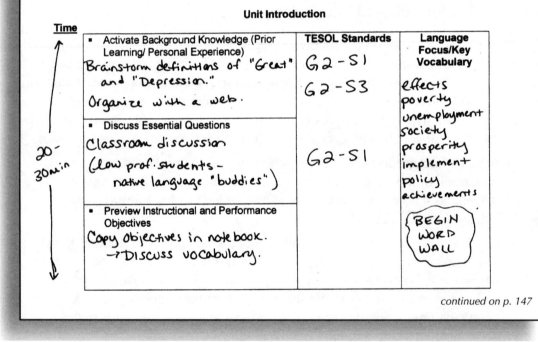

Time		TESOL Standards	Language Focus/Key Vocabulary
20–30 min	• Activate Background Knowledge (Prior Learning/ Personal Experience) Brainstorm definitions of "Great" and "Depression." Organize with a web.	G2–S1 G2–S3	effects poverty unemployment society prosperity implement policy achievements
	• Discuss Essential Questions Classroom discussion (low prof. students – native language "buddies")	G2–S1	
	• Preview Instructional and Performance Objectives Copy objectives in notebook. →Discuss vocabulary.		BEGIN WORD WALL

continued on p. 147

- Practice and apply: After encountering new information, students need the opportunity to work with it. A combination of group and individual work is ideal, with a wide variety of activities used throughout the unit. Appropriate activities for cooperative groups include role plays; information-gap activities; jigsaw activities; peer tutoring; problem solving; simulation; and the creation of a poster, cartoon, song, poem, debate, skill builder, or play. Appropriate activities for individual work include completing a graphic organizer; doing textbook exercises; keeping a double-entry reading log; doing process writing; completing a creative activity, such as a poster,

Unit Chart, *continued*

Unit: __10__

Performance Objective # ____1____

Performance Objective:

Explain the factors which caused the Great Depression

Time		TESOL Standards	Language Focus/Key Vocabulary
15 min.	▪ Activate Background Knowledge personal: Do you know someone who is unemployed? Why do people lose their jobs? prior learning: Describe the U.S. economy in the 1920's. What were the economic risks that people took?	G1-S2	
5-10 min.	▪ Preview Objectives and Lesson Prereading strategies: Title, headings, captions, graphics	G2-S3	
30-40 min.	▪ Discover Content / Learn Skill Discovery learning Activity: Assign 1 cause per group Find 3 key content words	G2-S3 G2-S1	past tense sentences Vocab: stock speculate production consumption regulate unemployment consumer wage depression
20-30 min.	▪ Practice and Apply Student presentations Student outlines	G2-S1 G2-S2	
Homework →	▪ Evaluate Cooperative group checklist presentations, outlines Journal entry: Most important cause	G1-S3 G2-S2	(also- student generated words from reading) ADD TO WORD WALL
10 min.	▪ Expand "Buying stocks" activity using newspaper + current stock prices		

continued on p. 148

cartoon, song, or poem; keeping a character diary; keeping a journal; and writing an authentic document (e.g., a newspaper article).

- Evaluate: We use a wide variety of assessment techniques throughout the lesson for each performance objective. This box on the chart can be used to record the forms of ongoing and final assessment. Appropriate assessment techniques include evaluating the final draft of the writing process; giving a formal quiz or test; having the students complete a sequence or time line; using a rubric; having the students complete peer or self-evaluations; having the students explain, justify, or summarize; having the students complete a

Unit Chart, *continued*

Unit Conclusion

Time		TESOL Standards	Language Focus/Key Vocabulary
15 min.	▪ Discuss Essential Questions Think / Pair / Share	G3 – S1 G3 – S2 G2 – S1	Review WORD WALL
20 min.	▪ Review Objectives Pair review – Brainstorm activities done for each objective – Find areas for review	G2 – S2	
3 days	▪ Final Project/Exam Research Project: "New Deal Programs that are Alive Today"	G2 – S2 G2 – S3	Topic Sentences Summarizing
1 day (optional)	▪ Expand Field Trip: FDR memorial Check stock progress from day 1	G1 – S1 G1 – S2	

Notes:

– Next year → Create simplified version of <u>Hard Times</u> excerpts for beginners.

– Allow more time for research project.

– Stock market activity & matching problems w/solutions went <u>GREAT</u>!

K-W-L chart; correcting or having the students correct written materials; and using a checklist. See also *Scenarios for ESL Standards-Based Assessment* (TESOL, in press).

- Expand: Here, the students have the opportunity to connect what they have learned to their personal experience, to current events, or to what they are learning in other subject areas. Appropriate activities include writing a letter to the editor, taking a field trip, doing community service, conducting an interview, writing a diary entry, or doing a current events activity (e.g., debating the involvement of government in social issues).

RESOURCES AND REFERENCES

Social Studies Textbooks Suitable for ESOL Students

Bernstein, V. (1992). *America: Su historia.* Austin, TX: Steck-Vaughn.

Bernstein, V. (1995). *America's story.* Austin, TX: Steck-Vaughn.

Bernstein, V. (1997). *America's history: Land of liberty.* Austin, TX: Steck-Vaughn.

Christison, M. S., & Bassano, S. (1993). *Social studies: Content and learning strategies.* Reading, MA: Addison-Wesley.

Hughes, G. E., Miller, N. D., & Volkening, S. L. (1983). *Reading American history: Getting the main idea, learning the vocabulary, reading maps and graphs.* Glenview, IL: Scott, Foresman.

Garcia, J., Harley, S., & Howard, J. (1995). *One nation, many people.* Paramus, NJ: Globe Fearon.

Harrington, K. L. (1993). *America: Past and present.* Boston: Heinle & Heinle.

McClanahan, S. D., & Green, J. A. (1996). *Building strategies: Social studies.* Austin, TX: Steck-Vaughn.

O'Connor, J. R. (1994). *Exploring American history.* Paramus, NJ: Globe Fearon.

Schwach, H. J. (1987). *Foundations in American history.* New York: Globe.

Suter, J. (1994). *United States history* (2nd ed.). Paramus, NJ: Globe Fearon.

Terdy, D. (1986). *Content area ESL: Social studies.* Palatine, IL: Linmore.

Other Classroom Resources

ABC News. (1998). 1929–1936: Stormy weather [Video segment]. In *The century: Decades of change.* (Available from Films for the Humanities, P.O. Box 2053, Princeton, NJ 08543, 800-257-5126)
> Stormy Weather *is a concise documentary of the highlights of the Great Depression that holds students' attention.*

Bernhard, V., Burner, D., Fox-Genovese, E., Genovese, E. D., McClymer, J., & McDonald, F. (1991). *Firsthand America: A history of the United States.* St. James, NY: Brandywine Press.
> *An advanced history text with many primary documents, this work serves as both a teacher resource and a source for adaptable material.*

Guthrie, W. (n.d.). This land is your land. In *The Asch recordings: Vol. 1* [Compact disc]. Washington, DC: Smithsonian Folkways.
> *This song is the classic American folk song.*

Moulton, C. (1996). Dust bowl journey. In *Eight plays of United States history* (pp. 107–131). Upper Saddle River, NJ: Globe Fearon Educational.
> *These plays are fictional representations of historical events that students can act out. They are accessible to intermediate- and advanced-level ESOL students.*

Slater, B. (1981). *History, economics, political science: Glossary of terms.* San Diego, CA: Dormac.
> *Hundreds of social studies terms are defined in simple language with understandable examples.*

Takaki, R. (1993). *A different mirror: A history of multicultural America.* Boston: Little, Brown.
> *This examination of U.S. history reflects the racial and cultural diversity of the nation.*

Terkel, S. (1970). *Hard times: An oral history of the Great Depression.* New York: Simon & Schuster.
> *This work consists of first-person accounts from people who lived through the Great Depression. The interviews are categorized by topic.*

Zinn, H. (1980). *A people's history of the United States.* New York: HarperCollins.
> *This account retells U.S. history from the perspective of people who have been traditionally left out of textbooks. It pays special attention to those who have been politically and economically marginalized.*

Teacher References

Adamson, L. G. (1998). *Literature connections to American history, K–6: Resources to enhance and entice*. Englewood, CO: Libraries Unlimited.
> *A comprehensive list of stories, poems, songs, and other literature, this work is suitable for secondary ESOL students. It includes suggestions for integrating its contents with U.S. history lessons.*

Brinton, D. M., & Masters, P. (Eds.). (1997). *New ways in content-based instruction*. Alexandria, VA: TESOL.
> *Offering a variety of ready-to-use lessons submitted by ESL classroom teachers, this work covers a range of ways to approach content instruction.*

Chamot, A. U., & O'Malley, J. M. (1994). *The CALLA handbook: Implementing the cognitive academic language learning approach*. Reading, MA: Addison-Wesley.
> *This approach to designing and planning lessons integrates content and language instruction with learning strategies.*

Crandall, J. (1987). (Ed.) *ESL through content area instruction: Mathematics, science, social studies*. Englewood Cliffs, NJ: Regents/Prentice Hall.
> *This work provides an introduction to the theory and practice of content-based instruction.*

Galt, M. F. (1992). *The story in history: Writing your way into the American experience*. New York: Teachers and Writers Collaborative.
> *This work recounts one teacher's experience of integrating writing and U.S. history.*

Giese, J. R., & Singleton, L. R. (1989). *United States history: A resource book for secondary schools*. Santa Barbara, CA: ABC-CLIO.
> *This resource book provides a wide variety of background information and resources available for history teachers.*

Goldstein, A. P. (1980). *Skillstreaming the adolescent*. Champaign, IL: Research Press.
> *This work offers interactive social skills training lessons for high school students.*

Hyser, R. M., & Arndt, J. C. (1995). *Voices of the American past: Documents in United States history* (Vol. 2). Orlando, FL: Harcourt Brace College.
> *This comprehensive collection of annotated primary sources can be adapted for ESOL students.*

Kagan, S. (1994). *Cooperative learning*. San Clemente, CA: Author.
> *Kagan's work is the authoritative guide to cooperative learning practices and activities.*

Kintisch, S., & Cordero, W. (1993). *Breaking away from the textbook: A new approach to teaching American history*. Lancaster, PA: Technomic.
> *This work offers innovative lesson ideas for creative teaching.*

Loewen, J. W. (1995). *Lies my teacher told me: Everything your American history textbook got wrong*. New York: New Press.
> *A critical examination of high-school U.S. history textbooks, this work points out myths, inaccuracies, and omissions prevalent among the most prominent texts.*

McElvane, R. S. (1984). *The Great Depression: America, 1929–1941*. New York: Times Books.
> *This work provides a comprehensive history of the period and can be used by teachers for their own background knowledge.*

Montgomery County Public Schools. (1992). *United States History B* [Curriculum]. (Available from Department of Academic Programs, Office for Instruction and Program Development, Montgomery County Public Schools, Carver Educational Services Center, 850 Hungerford Drive, Rockville, MD 20850)

Montgomery County Public Schools. (1998). *ESOL Level 3* [Curriculum]. (Available from Department of Academic Programs, Office for Instruction and Program Development, Montgomery County Public Schools, Carver Educational Services Center, 850 Hungerford Drive, Rockville, MD 20850)

National Center for History in the Schools. (n.d.). *National standards for United States history: Exploring the American experience*. Los Angeles: University of California.

Richards, J. C., Platt, J., & Platt, H. (1992). *Dictionary of language teaching and applied linguistics* (2nd ed.). Harlow, England: Longman.

This dictionary can serve as a sourcebook for teachers.

Short, D. (1991). *How to integrate language and content instruction: A training manual.* Washington, DC: Center for Applied Linguistics.

This work includes basic strategies and is especially suitable for teachers new to content-based instruction.

Teachers Curriculum Institute. (1994). *History alive! Engaging all learners in the diverse classroom.* Menlo Park, CA: Addison-Wesley.

Presenting the theory and practice of an innovative approach to teaching U.S. history, this work uses experiential learning and critical thinking activities.

TESOL. (1997). *ESL standards for Pre-K–12 students.* Alexandria, VA: Author.

TESOL. (in press). *Scenarios for ESL standards-based assessment.* Alexandria, VA: Author.

Glossary of Techniques

Procedures often vary somewhat from teacher to teacher. The following descriptions represent one widely accepted variant, but implementation may change depending on the teacher and the context.

Clock of partners: A quick way to put students in random pairs to work in class.

- Give each student a paper clock. Have the students write one classmate's name in each space corresponding to the 12 hours of the clock.

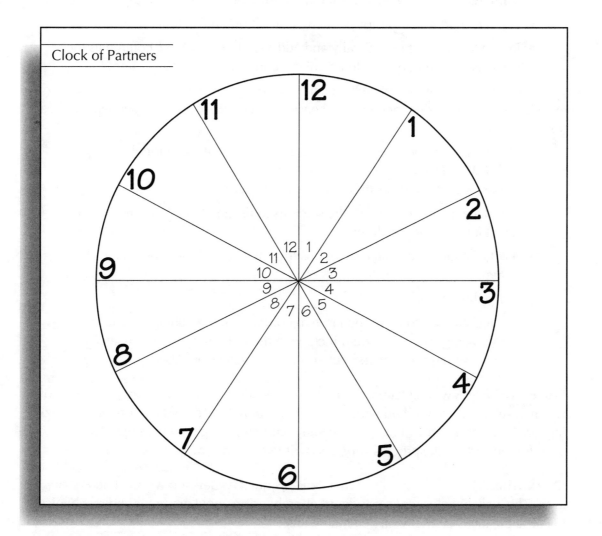

Clock of Partners

- Tell the students to keep the clocks in their binders and take them out when they are supposed to work in pairs.
- Give instructions for an assignment, and then announce what "time" it is. The students then consult their clocks to see which partner they will work with.

Cubing: A prewriting activity in which the writer looks at an idea from six angles, as if it were placed on a cube.

K-W-L chart: A chart used to help students access prior knowledge about a particular topic (what I *k*now), ask questions about the topic (what I *w*ant to know), and record what they have learned (what I *l*earned). A K-W-L chart may be done by the class as a group, with the teacher recording the information on a large chart on the chalkboard or on poster paper. This technique is often used to record what students are learning throughout a unit.

- Introduce the topic and have the students brainstorm what they already know about it. Record their ideas in the *K* column.
- Ask the students to think of things they would like to learn about the topic. Record their questions in the *W* column.
- Elicit suggestions for how the students could learn the things they want to learn. As they later gather this information, write it in the *L* column.
- Use the chart as a basis for planning instruction on this topic.
- Return to the chart periodically and add to it, filling in the *L* column as the students discover answers to any of the questions in the *W* column.

When the students complete the chart individually as part of a lesson, it is an excellent way of assessing their comprehension of a concept and independent application of new strategies.

- On the day you begin a new lesson, give the students a four-column sheet with *K-W-L-H* at the top. In the *H* column, the students will record resources and strategies they use (*how* I learned).
- Introduce the topic, and ask the students to list anything they already know about it under the *K* column.
- Ask the students to list the questions they have about the topic in the *W* column.
- Teach the lesson.
- Ask the students to fill in the last two columns after teaching your lesson, emphasizing that they should include in the last column not only the resources they encountered but also any strategies they used.

Process writing: A writing technique that guides students through the various stages of writing used by accomplished writers. The stages may include brainstorming, organizing, drafting, editing, rewriting, proofreading, and preparing the final copy. The terms used for the parts of the process vary, and writers vary in how they use the process.

Quickwrite: A technique used to generate ideas quickly, develop writing fluency, or both. The activity helps reduce students' apprehension about grammar and mechanics because the focus is strictly on generating ideas.

- Give the students a short, limited amount of time to write silently on a specific topic, statement, or question. Make it clear to the students that they will not be graded for content or grammar.

- After the students have finished, use the quickwrite as a springboard for further conversation, classroom activities, or an expanded writing process.

- Optionally, do this activity as a game in which the students are required to keep their pens or pencils moving at all times, even if it means writing something like "I can't think of anything to write."

Show, don't tell: Write in a way that includes dialogue and specific details and lets the readers discover how the characters feel from their actions and words.

Silent dialogue: Written conversation between two or more students.

- Have the students take turns writing their names in the left margin of a piece of paper.

- Ask the students to respond to and reflect on a preselected theme in the space next to their names. The resulting dialogue looks like a script for a play.

- If you wish, use the silent dialogue as a free-writing, shared activity.

Think/pair/share: An activity designed to give students an opportunity to reflect on any topic and briefly share their thoughts with a partner (see also Kagan, 1994).

- Assign the students a brief topic to think or write about individually. This usually works best in the form of a question or series of questions.

- To encourage the students to summarize their thoughts orally rather than reading aloud or reading their partners' work, collect the papers before the next step in the activity. Collecting the papers can also provide a fast and easy way to divide the students into partners: Mix up the collected papers, and randomly assign partners based on the location of the students' papers in the stack.

- Have the students share their ideas with an assigned partner. Depending on the context and goals of the lesson, have the students choose their partners, or assign them, either randomly or based on some criterion (e.g., academic level or native language).

- Conclude by asking the students to share with the whole class what they learned from their partner.

Webbing: A prewriting activity in which the writer arranges ideas to resemble a spider web. The writer places a central concept in the middle and related or supporting ideas extend outward.

Word wall: A list of the basic and most important words in a unit or a course, generally intended for use as a basis for language teaching or for the preparation of teaching materials (adapted from Richards, Platt, & Platt, 1992).

- Either create the list and present it to the students, or ask the students to identify words in a text or theme which they wish to learn.

- Post the words on the classroom wall on posterboard or on individual word cards that can be alphabetized.

A wide variety of activities, such as memory games, picture drawing, and charades, can be implemented using these words throughout the unit.

REFERENCES

Kagan, S. (1994). *Cooperative learning.* San Clemente, CA: Author.

Richards, J. C., Platt, J., & Platt, H. (1992). *Dictionary of language teaching and applied linguistics* (2nd ed.). Harlow, England: Longman.

About the Editors and Writers

Barbara Agor, editor of this volume, is a recently retired ESOL teacher in the Rochester City School District, New York. During her 34-year career, she also taught in India as part of a Fulbright grant, at the State University of New York at Brockport, at the University of Rochester, and at Nazareth College. She holds a BA, MA, and EdD from the University of Rochester. She has written many books and articles, some for students and others for colleagues, on topics such as computers in instruction, first and second language learning, and educational reform. She has been an active member of TESOL and New York State TESOL.

Sandra Briggs teaches in the San Mateo Union High School District in California, having started as a Spanish teacher, then becoming an ESL teacher, department chair, and district ESL coordinator. She did her undergraduate work at Pomona College and earned an MA in TESOL at San Francisco State University, an MAT from Johns Hopkins University, and an MA in linguistics from Stanford University. She has worked in curriculum development as well as in staff development for both ESL teachers and mainstream teachers who work with ESL students. She has coauthored a number of EFL/ESL texts for Scott, Foresman. In San Mateo, she has incorporated TESOL's ESL standards with California's ESL standards to revise the district's ESL program. She recently served on the TESOL Board of Directors.

George Bunch taught intermediate-level ESL, U.S. history, and government at John F. Kennedy High School in Montgomery County, Maryland, while he was writing his unit for this book. He earned an MA from the University of Maryland, Baltimore County, after having taught English in Venezuela and Spanish in a private school. He is currently pursuing a PhD in educational linguistics at Stanford University.

Ellen Daniels teaches at Wheaton High School in Montgomery County, Maryland. She received an MA in ESOL from the University of Massachusetts at Amherst, with a concentration in multicultural education and certification in social studies, Grades 9–12. She has taught ESL Levels 1, 2, and 3 along with sheltered U.S. history, basic reading (literacy), and sheltered math classes. She has also been involved in curriculum development for Hispanic high school students with limited literacy.

Patricia Hartmann teaches ESL at Charles F. Brush High School and Memorial Junior High School in the South Euclid–Lyndhurst School District, Ohio. She received a BA in Russian from Ohio State University and subsequently earned her MA and TESOL certificate, also from Ohio State University. She has incorporated the ESL standards into the development of K–12 math and social studies courses of study in her district. In 1999, she took part in a presentation at the 33rd Annual TESOL Convention on how different districts have incorporated the standards into their curriculum and teaching.

Suzanne Irujo, editor of this series, has taught ESL at all grade levels and spent many years teaching methodology and language acquisition courses and supervising ESL student teachers at Boston University. Her BA is in Spanish, her EdM is in bilingual education, and her EdD is in second language acquisition. She is semiretired, dividing her time between consulting on and editing ESL-related projects and enjoying the New Hampshire woods.

Carrie Lenarcic teaches social studies content classes in Manhattan Comprehensive Night and Day High School in New York City. She received a BA in English/anthropology from Hobart/William Smith Colleges and an MA from Teachers College, Columbia University. She has taught in Taiwan and has worked on the TESOL certification assessments for the National Board for Professional Teaching Standards.

William Pruitt has taught ESL and social studies since 1989 to middle and high school students at the Board of Cooperative Educational Services in western Monroe County, New York. He earned a BA in English from the University of Missouri and an MS in TESOL from the University of Rochester. In addition to his teaching, he is a professional storyteller and poet whose poems have appeared in such publications as *Ploughshares* and *Country Journal.*

Gwen Riles teaches intermediate-level ESL and global history at Manhattan Comprehensive Night and Day High School in New York City. She earned a BA in ancient history from Swarthmore College and spent 4 years teaching ESL in Tokyo. She completed her MA in TESOL at Teachers College, Columbia University.

Cynthia Ross teaches ESL at Chantilly High School in Fairfax County, Virginia. She received a BA in literature/writing from the University of California, San Diego, and an MA and secondary certification from George Mason University.

Users' Guide

Volume and Unit

Grade Levels	Pre-K–2						3–5						6–8						9–12					
	1	2	3	4	5	6	1	2	3	4	5	6	1	2	3	4	5	6	1	2	3	4	5	6
Pre-K	X																							
Kindergarten		X	X																					
Grade 1			X	X																				
Grade 2			X	X	X	X																		
Grade 3			X					X		X	X													
Grade 4							X		X	X														
Grade 5							X					X								X				
Grade 6													X	X		X	X		X					
Grade 7															X	X	X		X					
Grade 8															X	X	X		X					
Grade 9																			X	X	X		X	X
Grade 10																			X	X	X		X	X
Grade 11																			X	X	X	X	X	X
Grade 12																			X	X		X	X	X

Language Proficiency Levels	Pre-K–2						3–5						6–8						9–12					
	1	2	3	4	5	6	1	2	3	4	5	6	1	2	3	4	5	6	1	2	3	4	5	6
Beginning	X	X	X	X	X			X	X				X	X	X		X			X				X
Intermediate	X	X		X	X	X	X	X		X	X	X	X	X	X	X	X	X	X	X	X	X	X	X
Advanced	X	X			X	X	X		X		X	X	X		X	X		X	X					X
Native Speaker	X	X			X	X	X							X										

Program Models	Pre-K–2						3–5						6–8						9–12					
	1	2	3	4	5	6	1	2	3	4	5	6	1	2	3	4	5	6	1	2	3	4	5	6
Pull-out ESL[1]			X	X				X	X	X	X	X	X											
Departmentalized ESL[2]							X								X	X						X	X	
Intensive English[3]																				X				
Sheltered English[4]																X	X			X				X
Inclusion/Push-in ESL[5]		X				X																		
Team Teaching[6]													X							X				
Mainstream Class[7]	X			X			X						X											

Language and Content Areas	Pre-K–2						3–5						6–8						9–12					
	1	2	3	4	5	6	1	2	3	4	5	6	1	2	3	4	5	6	1	2	3	4	5	6
Basic Academic Skills	X	X	X	X																				
Listening and Speaking	X	X	X	X	X	X	X	X	X	X	X	X	X	X	X	X	X	X	X	X	X	X	X	X
Reading			X		X	X	X	X	X	X	X	X	X	X		X	X		X				X	X
Writing			X	X	X	X		X	X	X	X	X	X		X	X	X	X	X	X	X	X	X	X
Social Studies			X		X	X	X	X	X	X	X	X	X			X			X					X
Science		X		X								X	X	X			X			X				
Mathematics		X		X		X						X		X						X				

Standards	Pre-K–2						3–5						6–8						9–12					
	1	2	3	4	5	6	1	2	3	4	5	6	1	2	3	4	5	6	1	2	3	4	5	6
Goal 1, Standard 1	X	X		X	X	X	X		X			X	X		X		X		X					X
Goal 1, Standard 2	X	X	X		X	X		X					X		X	X			X	X				
Goal 1, Standard 3	X	X		X	X	X	X	X						X					X	X	X	X		X
Goal 2, Standard 1	X	X	X	X	X	X	X		X	X	X	X	X		X	X	X	X	X			X	X	X
Goal 2, Standard 2	X	X	X	X	X	X	X	X	X	X	X	X	X	X	X	X	X	X	X	X	X	X	X	X
Goal 2, Standard 3	X		X	X	X	X	X		X	X	X		X	X	X		X	X	X	X	X	X	X	X
Goal 3, Standard 1			X	X	X	X	X			X	X	X	X	X	X		X	X	X	X	X			X
Goal 3, Standard 2			X	X							X	X		X	X				X					X
Goal 3, Standard 3		X			X	X						X		X	X					X				

[1] ESOL students spend most of their time in a single classroom and are "pulled out" of that classroom for ESL.

[2] Students rotate from one class to another; the ESL class is one of many regularly scheduled classes at a particular time.

[3] The focus is on fast acquisition of language skills, whether in a pull-out, departmentalized, or self-contained class.

[4] ESOL students are taught English through or in conjunction with another subject, such as science or social studies.

[5] The ESL teacher goes into a mainstream class to work with students; activities may be separately or jointly planned and conducted.

[6] The ESL teacher and content or grade-level teacher are both responsible for the class.

[7] ESOL students are placed in a grade-level classroom with both native and nonnative speakers.

Teaching and Learning Strategies	Pre-K–2						3–5						6–8						9–12					
	1	2	3	4	5	6	1	2	3	4	5	6	1	2	3	4	5	6	1	2	3	4	5	6
Computer Skills		X					X				X	X	X	X		X	X	X			X			X
Cooperative Learning				X	X				X	X					X	X			X		X			X
Critical Thinking				X					X							X				X				X
Independent Research		X						X			X		X			X	X	X						X
Literature	X	X	X	X		X	X				X									X		X		
Learning Styles	X	X		X	X			X					X	X										
Parent Involvement	X		X		X			X																
Scientific Method			X												X							X		
Use of L1							X		X		X	X				X	X	X			X			X

Themes and Topics	Pre-K–2						3–5						6–8						9–12					
	1	2	3	4	5	6	1	2	3	4	5	6	1	2	3	4	5	6	1	2	3	4	5	6
Animals				X																				
Building Community								X																X
Careers		X	X																					
Colonial Life									X							X								
Communities, Helpers	X		X		X		X			X						X								
Environment												X					X							
Exploration													X											
Family	X		X					X												X				
Games									X															
Geography								X		X			X						X					
History									X	X			X			X			X					X
Measurement															X						X			
Multiculturalism		X		X	X	X	X	X		X	X				X									
Native Americans				X			X																	
Nutrition		X																						
Religions, Values																	X		X					
Self	X					X	X			X													X	
Socialization	X	X								X														
Writing Genres								X								X	X						X	X

Also Available From TESOL

American Quilt: A Reference Book on American Culture
Irina Zhukova and Maria Lebedko

Common Threads of Practice:
Teaching English to Children Around the World
Katharine Davies Samway and Denise McKeon, Editors

ESL Standards for Pre-K–12 Students
TESOL

Implementing the ESL Standards for Pre-K–12 Students
Through Teacher Education
Marguerite Ann Snow, Editor

New Ways in Teaching English at the Secondary Level
Deborah J. Short, Editor

New Ways in Teaching Young Children
Linda Schinke-Llano and Rebecca Rauff, Editors

New Ways in Using Authentic Materials in the Classroom
Ruth E. Larimer and Leigh Schleicher, Editors

New Ways in Using Communicative Games in Language Teaching
Nikhat Shameem and Makhan Tickoo, Editors

New Ways of Classroom Assessment
James Dean Brown, Editor

Reading and Writing in More Than One Language:
Lessons for Teachers
Elizabeth Franklin, Editor

Teacher Education
Karen E. Johnson, Editor

Teaching in Action: Case Studies From Second Language Classrooms
Jack C. Richards, Editor

Training Others to Use the ESL Standards:
A Professional Developmental Manual
Deborah J. Short, Emily L. Gómez, Nancy Cloud, Anne Katz,
Margo Gottlieb, Margaret Malone

For more information, contact
Teachers of English to Speakers of Other Languages, Inc.
700 South Washington Street, Suite 200
Alexandria, Virginia 22314 USA
Tel 703-836-0774 • Fax 703-836-6447 • publications@tesol.org • http://www.tesol.org/